IE____

D1513109

Should I Quit?

Resilience for a turbulent world

Mike Gordon

MIKE GORDON

Published by Dreamstone Publishing

www.dreamstonepublishing.com

Copyright © 2016 by Mike Gordon

Epiphanies Life Strategy & Coaching

www.epiphanies.com.au

ISBN: 1925499065

ISBN 13: 978-1-925499-06-3

DISCLAIMER

The information, strategies, concepts, techniques and suggestions in this book are of a general nature only, and do not constitute, and are not intended as a substitute for, professional or individual advice in any way. You should consult with the appropriate qualified professionals (including psychologists, psychiatrists, counsellors, medical practitioners and other healthcare providers, insurance advisers, financial advisers, and legal advisers) and seek your own independent professional advice relating to your particular circumstances and needs.

Although the author and the publisher have made every effort to ensure that the contents of this book were accurate at press time, the author and the publisher do not represent or warrant their accuracy. The author and the publisher are not responsible for any disruption, loss or damage (including indirect or consequential damages) suffered by any party as a result of, or in relation to, the use of this book. To the extent permitted by law, the author and the publisher exclude any liability (including liability for negligence or other default) to any party for any disruption, loss or damage (including indirect or consequential damages) arising from or in relation to the use of this book.

Epiphanies Life Strategy & Coaching

DEDICATION

This book is dedicated to Michael, StJohn, Alexia, Gerry and April who supported me through my darkest times with their guidance, teaching and inspiration on how to live a resilient life.

And to my wonderful clients who have taught me much more about life, and myself, than I could ever learn from a text book.

Without them, this book could never have been written.

WHAT READERS ARE SAYING ABOUT THIS BOOK

"This is a great read. Well researched and deeply insightful. I felt like Mike was speaking directly to me and I have absorbed so much. I'm already putting his ideas into action in my own life. "

Tim Daly
Videographer and Web Designer

♦

"Mike's wise words astound me. I especially got a great reward from the practical exercises Mike assigns in the free Resilience Workbook download."

Ruth Vitek
Project Manager

♦

"Having previewed this work, I love it. It's a very helpful guide for those who are transitioning in any way, especially careers and jobs. Mike Gordon is easy to read, thorough, comprehensive, accessible and full of wisdom."

Michael Parise
Stress reduction and Trauma recovery practitioner

♦

"Interesting and useful approaches to many of life's big questions. Very actionable."

Brad Veitch
Technical Business Analyst

"Mike Gordon taps deep insights, while defining well researched and practical steps. His guidance on my life's purpose and design raises me above the humdrum and ordinary eking of existence."

Juliah Faith
Sound and Harmony Scientist

♦

"A great read. I was so absorbed I missed my train station and carried on to the next. No worries, I still managed to make it to work on time!"

Linda Allen
Customer Services Trainer

♦

"I share Mike Gordon's belief in the importance of resilience and flexibility - our environment is changing so rapidly and so frequently, and being fixed in our ways hinders not just us personally but the people we are trying to serve."

Serena Low
Midlife Career Mentor

♦

"I love this book. It has a whole new perspective on situations. It's full of really useful ideas that I can apply directly to my life and my business."

Andrew Killen
Craftsman and Retailer

TABLE OF CONTENTS

MIKE GORDON

FOREWORD

From Julian Noel: Shine Global

This is more a glowing fire, than a book. Many readers will be warmed by the wisdom in these pages.

We live in interesting times. Change is happening at a rate never experienced before. The roles of big business, politics and finance have altered forever.

The lines between local and global have blurred. These changes have been both liberating and shocking: and we now have to think differently. Many people have been caught off guard, and are uncertain of how to traverse this new landscape.

There is a growing trend for people to seek meaning from their work, and balance in their lives. Some are making new choices; some are having the choice made for them; the maelstrom of transition makes no distinction.

Thank heavens for Mike Gordon's book - it provides a template for a new way of seeing, and navigating, these times.

As a coach and facilitator, I meet many people who have made the choice to change their lives. Most want to express more of themselves through their work. Mike has written a manual for these brave souls.

At this time of transition, we need new perspectives. Einstein said, *"We cannot solve our problems with the same thinking we used when we created them."* We are asking different questions, and we seek meaning, as we trade time for money.

For many, transition is a painful and perilous experience. I have seen CEOs, doctors, public servants, and others flounder. Transition is an unmapped territory; an internal landscape, full of uncharted mountain ranges, rivers and oceans.

I once worked with a Doctor who, for 25 years, had unfailingly applied herself to being a GP. One day her perspective shifted, and she felt compelled to take a new direction in her life. She joined an international body of doctors serving in refugee camps around the world.

For 5 years she experienced a deep restlessness which took her all around the globe. Unsettled, her marriage suffered, she lost her house and her career was left on the rocks. For wont of such a book, I wonder how her journey might have been different.

There are more and more people transitioning. This book can bring immense solace and affirmation to them. Mike is the perfect person to have written this - he left his well-paid corporate job at the peak of his powers, when he had climbed the corporate ladder, attaining worldly success, with career highlights anyone would feel proud to have achieved.

Nonetheless, in his final year in corporate life, he could sense that change was on the horizon. He began to explore what a new life might look like. He saw departing workmates fail and succeed. He tells stories of the successful ones. His journey started with him sitting behind his all too familiar desk, until, one day, he was called into the office for a chat - 'The chat'. He was prepared. He set sail.

Mike has navigated this strange territory, climbed the mountains, visited the valleys, and has distilled and recorded his learnings into maps for us all to follow. Many people will be guided by his insights.

He covers great topics, resilience, demonstrating the difference between tough and strong, calling us to go deeper into our inner reserves of strength and encouraging us to remember that strength lives within us all. He speaks at length about intuition, and the pool of wisdom that resides in each of us. When we start to follow our life's calling, it is the intuition that guides us, and we must learn how to distinguish its voice from the chatter in our head.

He brings gentle 'art' back into the phrase, 'the art of decision making'. Learning to create a future worth living in is not something that we are trained to do.

We are trained to enter into systems - education, monetary, corporate life. Social norms guide our thinking, but, as the world changes, new paradigms are emerging, at times, seductively, at other times, catastrophically. It is a comfort to know that we can make different choices.

Mike goes a long way to providing a template for this new way of thinking.

Julian Noel

Founder of Shine - a global community of Entrepreneurs and pioneers creating a brighter future for all.

www.shineglobal.com.au

INTRODUCTION

If you're anything like me, you'll have experienced some pretty big changes in your life. Some will have been good and some will have been awful. But look around. You're still here!

The world didn't stop just because your circumstances changed or you had to move on. Life carried on, for better or worse, but it kept on going.

This book is all about making change work for the better, even if that means leaving your current situation, at home, at work, in business, or elsewhere.

It's about building your inner resilience to be able to cope with life and its changes. It'll encourage you to step back, review the situation and plan how the changes are going to go.

Perhaps you'll be able to improve your current situation, and make it good again, or maybe it will involve moving away and starting something new.

Either way, you'll see that quitting isn't a great option, when there are so many better ones available.

So welcome to 'Should I Quit?' and congratulations on making an investment in your own resilient future. I expect it will be a voyage of discovery and I trust you'll feel safe in my hands.

The information in this book has been gained from more than 40 years of my own career, my research into change and life planning and the direct experiences of my clients and of people that I have met in my mentoring practice.

But it isn't simply targeted at career planning. Anyone who's encountering any kind of life change will get value from this book.

You might be changing jobs, or considering ending a relationship.

You might be running your own business or association and wondering if it's still giving you value. Or it might be centred around a domestic situation, where you live, with family and friends.

In this book you'll find a wealth of practical wisdom on what resilience and values are. You'll also find a wide range of handy hints and tips to try in everyday life.

How would it feel to know that you had the ability to cope with any situation?

That you could learn to spot what value is, in our own terms?

That you could learn how to turn situations to the best outcomes for yourself?

Good? Then read on.

I've kept this book to the higher principles of change, resilience and value, to give as many people as much insight as I can. Of course, every reader will want to personalise the ideas for their own situation.

Wherever possible I'll include real-life examples, where others have tackled difficult situations and have come out winning. These could be from my own life, or from my clients and other people I've encountered along the way. The examples are included to demonstrate that ordinary people can do extraordinary things and that you are one of those people.

To help with this, I've created a downloadable 'Resilience Workbook': a series of exercises and planners, to help you to review the book's ideas, as they relate to you personally. I've compiled it in association with Epiphanies, my life strategy and coaching practice. Each chapter in this book explores new ideas and there's a worksheet associated with each one.

You'll find a link to the Resilience Workbook download page at the end of every chapter. The password that you will need, to unlock your access to the workbook, is at the end of Chapter 12.

Feel free to download it at any time... it's my gift to you, to reward you for committing to yourself, and to thank you for investing in 'Should I Quit?'

So do be prepared to put in some additional work beyond simply reading this. Be prepared to grow, to change and to flourish. There is no such thing as a free lunch, but this book is designed to feed you for life, with just a little effort from yourself.

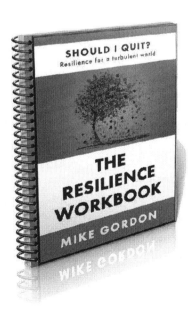

Why trust Mike Gordon?

Let me be absolutely clear. I am not a guru. I do not sit under a banyan tree in the wilderness, dispensing words of wisdom to acolytes. No, instead, I am a busy and very hands-on mentor and life coach.

I spend my days helping other people, my clients, to find their own purpose, develop their own life goals and work their plan to achieve the lives they want. In all of that, resilience, not dogged determination, is a key component to a turnaround.

What I've learned about resilience I have picked up, in part, from studying text books, but mostly from real life: from my own renaissance (more of that later) and the experience of many, many clients over the years.

I often say to people that I'm in the 'light bulb' business. You know, those times when someone simply 'gets it' - where the realisation hits, where the veil falls away, where the metaphorical bulb on top of their head lights up. Those are the moments I've worked for, all my life, and to which I am now dedicated. This book is a distillation of those moments in other people, and in myself.

As a single personal example, come with me back to 2012.

You'd see a grey meeting room, in a grey office building on a very grey mid-week day. Everything in the room had seen better days and looked tired. If you weren't depressed before you came in with me, you could well be now.

I'm sitting at one side of the table and opposite me are two other people; one, a lady of 'a certain age', wearing loose-fitting clothes and comfortable shoes. She had a stack of papers in manila folders and was shuffling them studiously. The other person was a 'young buck' junior executive in shiny black shoes, a shiny suit, a stiff collared shirt and tie, and more hair gel than a 1950s head waiter in a grand hotel.

He held a single sheet of paper, with a few salient bullet points about the state of the economy, the downturn in business and the need to re-balance costs. In short, I was being 'let go', 'downsized', 'made redundant' and, my personal favourite, 'retrenched'.

As he was making all his points on the necessity of my imminent ejection from the bosom of the firm's embrace, the HR lady was passing over a series of papers for my inspection and signature. "Separation package", she called it.

It was clear this was a difficult situation for them, as they shifted and squirmed in their seats. I saw very little value, to me, in making this performance any easier for them.

I merely sat quietly and listened to all they had to say. I reviewed their documents carefully and duly signed them in the places marked with those stick-on arrows that officials love to use. Finally, they advised that the 'separation' would take immediate effect but that I had a few days to clear my desk and return all working papers and electronic equipment.

Actually, there was no need for those few days. At the end of the formalities, I simply reached into my briefcase and took out my laptop computer and mobile telephone. Stuck to them was a sticky note with all the relevant access codes and passwords for the computer and the multitude of business applications I used. Likewise, the phone. In addition, I had a form from my local telco for a 'transfer of number'. I would be leaving their contract but taking the phone number with me.

The pair opposite were fairly surprised by my composure and readiness for this calamity.

They realised, as did I, that this was probably the end of my corporate career. In usual circumstances, it would represent catastrophic change for most people. What they didn't realise was that this was precisely what I had been working towards, for the past six to nine months.

My work never faltered, but my levels of dissatisfaction were made ever more obvious. In short, I wanted to go, but I wasn't going for free.

Through various conversations, I had let it be known that I would consider voluntary redundancy, if and when such a budget was available and they might be looking for volunteers.

That day came, I was put on the list and the axe fell.

At the end of the meeting I stood up, thanked them for their clarity and directness, thanked the company (through them) for the amazing opportunities the past 16 years had given me, and acknowledged how difficult that final meeting must have been for them. I shook their hands warmly, smiled, and left.

I walked directly out of the building and into the sunlight. The metaphor of stepping out of the grey corporate interior into the Sydney technicolour daylight did not escape me. My whole life was moving back into full colour.

It was precisely at that moment I realised just how resilient I had become. I had been under unwelcome pressure, but I'd taken the long view and engineered an outcome I wanted. I had not snapped in two. I had not been shaken into a heap of rubble. I was alive, well and ready for the next chapter in my life.

Now don't get me wrong, I was not always so resilient. There had been earlier times where major disruptions had broken me. Other job changes, breaking up and separating from the love of my life and a move from London to Sydney were all fairly traumatic and I didn't handle them well.

I guess the biggest difference this time, was that I had learned what true resilience is, I had built it up within myself and was able to exercise it in my favour.

And that's the purpose of this book: to help you, my valued reader, to achieve the same for yourself.

How to use this book

OK, we've laid down some broad strokes on what this book is all about and how it works. In this book you will be learning about resilience and how to get it, develop and maintain it. These pages contain a wealth of insights and practical actions that you can take. It might be too big to digest in a single sitting, so don't try.

Rather than being a single dish, think of it as a whole menu for a longer journey; the journey to a new you. It contains complete meals and lots of snacks for the trip.

Be selective:

- Dip in and out.

- Read a single chapter and begin to embrace what resonates with you.

- Do some simple thought exercises and turn them into real-life practice.

- Download the workbook and use the sheets to clarify your thinking and guide your activity.

My intention is to keep it light and well-paced; to be direct without being overbearing or pushy. Go through it in your own time and the sequence of your priority issues. But go through it all over time. Rome wasn't built in a day. Neither will your resilience be.

Don't forget the free Resilience Workbook. You'll find a link to it at the end of each chapter. It's designed to give you an opportunity to review your own experience and to take personal action to improve your own life.

You'll find a worksheet related to each chapter and the whole collection will combine to give you a decisive plan, to improve your own resilience, by understanding your value and values. Think of it as free life coaching from an expert professional.

Simply follow the link and download your own free copy.

So, well done, you've taken the first step in building your own resilience, and managing the changes in your life. It'll take some thought and some personal dedication. I hope you'll find it valuable. Most of all, I hope you enjoy this book.

Remember to download your free

Resilience

Workbook

Just follow the link below.

http://mikegordonbooks.com/download-sig-workbook/

You'll need the password that you find, at the end of Chapter 12

CHAPTER 1: QUITTING OR CHANGING?

We've all been there, haven't we? The feeling that we've reached the end of the road, or that we can't handle things any more. We reckon something... anything... has got to be better than this.

Am I right?

That's the point when we begin to consider jumping ship. Our instincts say *"Let's just get out of here,"* and we scarcely stop to think that there might be a better way to handle these times.

When we're at a turning point like this, our emotions are usually flaring. Our adrenalin begins to drive our primordial instincts into 'fight or flight'. We begin to lash out and we all know how that can end. It's never good. So, can we aim for a better outcome than simply running away?

Then, here's another twist. There's the old saying that 'as one door closes another opens.' ... and that usually implies 'into the unknown'. In my view, that's nearly right, but not completely.

Firstly, life is continuous and doesn't give us breaks of nothingness. So the door that's closing, and the door that's opening, is the same door. As we step through, it's still our lives and they're not stopping just because we change something. Think of it like an interior door at home, from one room to the next. It's not an exterior door where we're leaving the world we know altogether.

Secondly, our lives are in our own control and nobody else's. Other people and situations might be a trigger for change, but it's only us who can decide how we handle it. If we set out to quit, without looking forward to what comes next, that's still our decision, under our control. Even when we think we're quitting, we're not actually quitting; we're simply choosing not to plan the change.

Thirdly, if change is under our control, we can choose how the change will go. We can decide whether we're simply moving away from something or positively moving towards something new. Yes, once again, it's our choice.

If change is going to happen and we control how it's going to unfold, we may as well choose to change for the better. Quitting leaves the outcome in the realms of chance, but choosing to move on is much more self-determined. If we're choosing to make a change, let's make it a good one ... and that's nothing like quitting.

So quitting is never really quitting. It's really all about changing - moving on from one situation to a better one; from one way of living to another; from one place, job, relationship or task to something more fulfilling. And, if change is the name of the game, then the strategies, plans and tactics become about improving our life, not simply ending things as they were. Suddenly, we're looking forward at new opportunities, rather than backwards, at some sticky situation.

Those turning points are precisely the points for us not to be jumping just anywhere. Instead, it's time to stop, take a step back and consider what's really going on. In that light, we should really be looking for alternative, and better, responses to our situation, rather than asking ourselves: *'Should I quit?'* Remember another old adage:

Act in haste, repent at leisure.

Sometimes, the answer will, indeed, turn out to be an emphatic *'Yes, let's move on'*. Sometimes it'll be a definite *'No'*.

At most other times it will be a qualified

'Well, maybe. Let's see if I can make things work better for me.'

All of a sudden, we've moved out of a reactive-response mode (fight or flight) and begun to call on our inner resilience: our ability to see all around an issue, to be flexible and to make the best of every situation.

I recognise that change is scary. Being flexible is hard, when every fibre of our being is screaming *'get out!'* Looking for improvements seems pointless, when we've already concluded that this situation is worthless. Stepping back, rather than out, can seem like prolonging the agony, rather than resolving it. Well, that's where this book comes in, so keep on reading.

We'll look at how we can re-frame our perspectives and learn to see the positive qualities of every situation. We'll learn how to negotiate tricky times (and people) and we'll learn to find the gems among the dirt.

Then, if we decide it is, indeed, time to move on, we'll look at how to do that successfully; on our terms and to our best advantage. Throughout, we'll be learning how to recognise, and develop, our resilience and harness it to get the best outcomes for ourselves, from every situation.

But this book is not about quitting, because I believe that, in reality, we can never really quit. It is about moving from merely surviving to thriving: from merely coping with life into making life what we want it to be. It's about extracting every drop of value from every situation and creating situations of even more value - value as we define it in situations that work best for us. It's about being resilient, not merely tough.

Also, be advised that resilience doesn't come for free. We all have resilience, but it needs us to recognise it; to find it, to develop it and to harness it for our own benefit. That will require some work from each of us and this book will show you how to do that, if you take the time and effort to get there.

The themes of change and resilience

I hope, by now, I have whetted your appetite for change. Not for quitting,, but for direct, positive and meaningful change. If I have, then we're halfway there.

As we go along, you'll find some recurring themes about change and resilience.

Watch out for them. See how often they crop up and in how many different situations.

It doesn't matter if you're wrestling with pressures at work, at home, with family or friends, - these truths remain constant.

No matter if it's stages of life, location, relationships, money or being stuck in a rut, the core elements of resilience prevail across the spectrum. The principles apply and it'll be our mission to apply them directly to our own circumstances.

Surprisingly, it's the ability to harness our resilience that will make us extraordinary. That brings me to the first theme. (and the others follow, below)

1. We all have inner resilience

The sad point is that most people don't realise it. We've all heard the urban legends of a grandmother lifting up a car to free a child.

Where did that come from? Did she know she could lift a car? No, instinct simply kicked in and there she was, lifting a car.

That strength was there, all the time, but totally hidden - what are your hidden strengths?

2. We usually learn about resilience when it's already too late

We all have our resilience within us. It's there, but, too often, we overlook it. When life is running smoothly we know how to cope and we roll along blissfully. It's only when adversity strikes that we look around for support and help.

Most often, we look outside ourselves for it. Who can help me out? When no external assistance is forthcoming, that's when we look inwards, to our own resources. Our needs drive a search for our own solutions and that's when our resilience comes to the fore. But what if it didn't need to be like that? What if we were already aware of our inner abilities?

That's simple: First, situations won't seem so catastrophic, when they arise, because we know that we can cope. Second, our own experience, of living through tough times, can give us the confidence that we'll survive this time. And finally, by being aware of our own values, we can most often head off difficulties before they even arise.

So knowing about our inner strength -- our resilience -- in advance is a great way to stay on an even course and weather the toughest storm.

3. Our resilience is founded on our own sense of purpose

By knowing what's right for us, we know what the best solution to any problem will be. We can take direct steps to make sure that any solutions and outcomes fit what we need and want. Let's be clear about our overall purpose and the context is set for a smooth and even life.

4. Change happens

So why is it such a surprise to us when it does? Our inability to cope with change is most often linked to our attachment to the status quo. By recognising that our resilience allows us to take unforeseen circumstances in our stride, we can be ready to take whatever is passed to us.

Being attached to our purpose lets us see what's really important and not to be too attached to the 'stuff' in our lives. Letting go, or embracing the new, becomes easier if we're aware of the context in which it sits. If it can no longer serve us, that's OK. There are plenty more options that we can choose. That's the basis of being flexible and adaptable to change.

5. Intuition is our best guide

Yes, that's right, intuition. In a modern life, we're constantly being bombarded with facts and figures; rules and regulations or 'shoulds', 'musts' and 'ought tos'. Our unconscious mind is the home of our values and purpose, and the repository of all of our experience. And our intuition is our unconscious mind's barometer.

Our conscious minds might forget what we did yesterday, but our unconscious mind never forgets and is always comparing new experiences with what we value and what went before. Our intuition is our early warning system for difficult situations in the making. If something doesn't feel right, then it's probably not. We can all hear the warning bells, but usually dismiss them in preference to toughing it out.

That's not resilience, that's doggedness and most often leads to the very disasters we'd prefer to avoid. Let's learn how to listen to, and trust, our intuition - our gut feelings - and continue to live the life we want.

6. Conscious decisions are the manifestation of resilience

Once we've heard the warning bells, and are aware that some action might be needed, that's the time to engage our conscious minds. We can easily review the situation against our true purpose, our real needs and our deepest desires.

We can evaluate options and decide how we're going to proceed: to stay, to go or to change what's there. These are all conscious activities, but they are based on the unconscious knowledge that we can deal with adversity and maintain a path to our true purpose.

7. And finally, this is our life

Other people may love us, and wish us well, but they will never be as invested in our wellbeing as we are ourselves. If we want a happy and purposeful life, it's our responsibility to decide what that is, to make it happen and to maintain it ourselves.

Expecting other people to care more about our lives than we do is not only a waste of time, but may actually do us harm. Of course, other people might care about us to some degree, but their own wellbeing will always come first.

I'm not suggesting open warfare between clashing desires - far from it. I am suggesting that any change needs to encompass gains on all sides.

We hear people (particularly bosses) talking about 'win-win' situations. They are looking out, most often, for their own 'win'. Your 'win' becomes little more than a 'nice to have' rather than a mandatory outcome. Remember, *self*-nurture is not *self*ishness.

Resilience: what is it?

I've been talking about resilience a fair amount so far, so let's be clear about it. I'm doing this simply to remove any nagging uncertainty, before I ask you to launch yourself into a programme of change and development.

I want to give you confidence in what we're talking about and to dispel any doubts about the source of the suggested plan of action. I do recommend this short section to help you get into a positive frame of mind before we embark on this journey, and to help you feel comfortable with me, as your travelling companion.

Dictionaries provide a first level of definition for resilience – on the opposite page you can see some dictionary definitions of the word. I've chosen these specific definitions, because I believe that they point to some inner qualities of a substance or person. Other definitions I've read, and so many of the 'self-help' gurus and the associated literature, prefer to focus on 'toughness, hardness or external shielding.'

I don't like those views, because I believe that they miss the fundamental point - that resilience is not about rigidity and unflinching hardness. Instead, it is a much more organic, intelligent and sympathetic quality, which allows us to bend and flex to external pressures, rather than snap.

With my coaching clients, I often use the analogy of an earthquake. We've all seen news coverage of the aftermath of some horrific earthquake. We see images of desolation, with buildings shaken to rubble all around.

But have you ever noticed anything of inspiration in those scenes? Among all the rubble, what's still standing? Invariably, you'll see a single tree standing there - up to its trunk in debris, but still there. Or wooden-framed buildings left intact, while their concrete and brick neighbours have collapsed. How come they survived?

RESILIENCE - Definitions:

➢ *The power or ability to return to the original form, position, etc., after being bent, compressed, or stretched; elasticity.*

➢ *Ability to recover readily from illness, depression, adversity, or the like; buoyancy.*

Dictionary.com

➢ *The capability of a strained body to recover its size and shape after deformation caused, especially by compressive stress.*

➢ *An ability to recover from, or adjust easily to, misfortune or change.*

Webster-Miriam Dictionary

➢ *The capacity to recover quickly from difficulties; toughness.*

Oxford English Dictionary

Simple: they bend! They have been shaped, over time by nature, or by mankind's learned experience, to move and flex with the upheaval

So, my take on resilience is not to be tough, hard or unyielding. Quite the opposite: I say resilience is about inner flexibility, adaptability and the ability to rebound. In this scenario, resilience is much more like a tree than a marble pillar.

In fact, since I've moved to Australia, I've been totally inspired by the eucalyptus trees: you can burn them, flood them, parch them in drought or blow whole limbs off them. But, in only a few short months, you'll see the green shoots of new, vibrant growth emerge and the tree begin to flourish once more. No marble pillar could ever recover itself like that.

In judo, we are taught to roll with the blows and use opposing power against itself; to be efficient in our own resources and harness the situation around us.

Medieval jousting, on the other hand, was all about adopting a position of strength and power to throw all you had at your opponent. Force was applied directly, and brutally, as an onslaught. The more powerful contender won, the less powerful was left broken and vanquished.

Sun Tzu, the ancient Chinese military philosopher, (quoted opposite) points to many truths about resilience, and the need to step back, understand and plan, before leaping into battle. His legendary wisdom centres around intelligence, and simple efficiencies, rather than brute strength.

I'm not suggesting that all of life is a war and that we become combatants in battle. Instead, I am suggesting that our greatest strength is in the ability not to go to battle with situations but, instead, to learn how to work external pressures for our own benefit.

Resilience is all about understanding who we are, what our strengths are, and what we really value, as a 'win' in our own lives.

"To fight and conquer in all our battles is not supreme excellence; supreme excellence consists in breaking the enemy's resistance without fighting."

Sun Tzu:
The Art of War

"He will win who knows how to handle both superior and inferior forces."

Sun Tzu:
The Art of War

Difficult situations are going on all around us, all the time. Very often, the external forces will be much stronger than us and a direct assault on them would be futile.

So, in this book we'll be talking a lot about knowing our own strengths and knowing what we value; about picking our battles and about choosing to harness situations,, rather than fighting them. That's where true resilience lies.

 **Remember to download your free**

Resilience

Workbook

Just follow the link below.

http://mikegordonbooks.com/download-sig-workbook/

You'll need the password that you find, at the end of Chapter 12

CHAPTER 2: LIFE IN A STRAIGHT LINE

"Life is a series of experiences, each one of which makes us bigger, even though sometimes it is hard to realise this. For the world was built to develop character, and we must learn that the setbacks and grieves which we endure help us in our marching onward."

- **Henry Ford**
Industrialist, Ford Motor Company

Over the three decades of my corporate career I was privileged to work with many world-class project managers. I learned great lessons from them and I value the insights that they gave me. A shared characteristic I noticed in them is that project managers like to think in straight lines.

They have a goal or an outcome and they have a starting point, they have resources (skilled people, budgets and time scales) and they have a plan.

Put them all together and you create a straight line path from the current state to the desired state. The project managers would then work tirelessly along the path which they had designed.

They would allow for parallel streams of activity but those would all be shaped to come together at key checkpoints. Progress toward their goals would be delineated as a linear progress from one checkpoint to the next, in a well-ordered sequence.

The very best of them would recognise that unforeseen circumstances might crop up, so they'd build in contingencies – a reserve of extra resources – which they could call on to tackle those unplanned hiccups. But their intention was always to get back onto their plan - their straight-line plan.

Well, life isn't simply a project with a starting point and a well-defined outcome. There is no hand-over to operational running. Life is all operational running, even if we have goals, resources and a plan. It keeps on going. Even if we create projects in our lives, to achieve specific goals, life carries on around them. From minute to minute, day to day, year to year, these are our lives.

All of it is life. There are no rehearsals, practice areas nor do overs. We can't isolate our development activities from our day-to-day living

What's more:-

"Nature abhors a straight line."

William Kent
Landscape garden architect, 1720.

Look around you. Where in nature do you see straight lines or square corners? No, nature is curved, bendy and branched. But it is also continuous: it doesn't stop or take time off for a break.

Life might not be a straight line, but it is continuous and doesn't have gaps. Yet in modern life we are encouraged to believe in straight lines. Our architecture, our time management and our goal-setting are all predicated on the principle of efficiency, the shortest distance between two points - the straight line.

Think about the way we traditionally talk about our lives. We go to school, then college, we get a job, get married, get promoted, have kids, get promoted, buy a bigger house, get promoted, retire, live happily ever after. A nice, neat, simple straight line.

And then real life happens! The kids come early, we don't land our dream job, we get extra workload without a pay rise, we lose our job and spend two years on the bench, the kids are ungrateful brats and don't move out when it's their time, we get sick, we get old and give up our sports or hobbies, we don't have enough money and we can't enjoy our retirement in the way that we had planned.

Yep, life has a way of messing up our beautifully straight-lined plans. So, rather than using a modular, or step-wise, building block model to life, I prefer to think in terms of life being more like a river - fluid, changing, adaptable and continuous. It carries on regardless of obstacles, gradient or terrain. Sometimes it will be fast and furious, as it hurtles down a steep mountain, sometimes it will be slow and lazy when the terrain is flat. Sometimes it will meet barriers and will totally change direction, maybe even doubling back for a while. Sometimes it will duck underground and re-emerge somewhere else, or drop over a cliff in freefall for a while. But it never stops: it keeps on going until it reaches its end in the ocean, or some vast lake.

What are we supposed to do with this situation? How do we live in a curvy world, with our straight-lined plans? The problem isn't with the curvy world, that's just how it is. The problem isn't with our plans; they're a perfectly sensible approximation of the direct path between two points.

No, the problem lies with us; with our expectations of life and our attachments to the 'self' we think we should be.

When real life steps in and brings its curves, we need to reconsider who we are, what we want and how we're actually going to get there.

In this chapter, we'll look at some new ways of looking at our plans, our expectations and life's curves, at how to live a real life, curves and all. We'll examine why plans are useful, but also how to avoid treating them as gospel. Most importantly, we'll look at how our inbuilt resilience can be brought to bear, and be developed, in these 'bendy' times.

Before we dive into the concept of life's resilience any further, let's first figure out if we have, or even want, a well-planned life plan or career. The dictionaries have a variety of definitions for the word 'career' but I suspect there are as many definitions out there as there are people trying to follow one. The same is true for a life plan.

There are, however, a few concepts that all the definitions agree upon:

- First, it's a series or progression of circumstances and events.

- Second, there is some sense of consistent focus and activity.

- Third, there is a notion of a definite direction or trajectory.

- Finally, there is some idea of speed along that trajectory.

To these elements I would add an idea so fundamental that it's often overlooked. That's the idea of a unifying goal to drive our progress. Of course, life or careers can have a variety of goals: To earn $XXX by a given time; to achieve a certain position; to build a secure home and family, to be recognised in our field; to retire with enough to live comfortably.

These all seem to have a point destination and a single, direct line of sight to it.

They can be considered as linear plans with linear goals. What's more, these linear careers can be vertical - the traditional climbing of the ladder to ever more advanced positions, or horizontal - where the drive and ambition move laterally to build skills, networks, influence and experience. Both these vertical and horizontal ambitions remain consistent with the notion of a career or life plan. Move from A to C, and if we need to go sideways through B to get there, the plan is still valid.

But do we still have a career or life plan if our goals are not linear? What if our goals or ambitions are always to be working at something we enjoy? To try different things. To feel fulfilled in everything we do. To stretch our boundaries and learn new things. These goals are much more about the here and now, about the life we're living at present, and much less focused on a destination. Can we have a non-linear set of jobs and circumstances, and still call it a career? Does it matter that our plan does not follow the classical vertical linear path?

I had a colleague, Bob, in my early career, who had reached the level of senior manager, but had stalled. It was clear that he wasn't likely to gain much more seniority, or salary, as an employee in a corporate firm. What's more, his marriage had also stalled and he drifted slowly into divorce. (Funny how that often happens.) He was reaching middle age, was middle management in his mid-career. Yet he was nowhere near 'mid-lifed'. His sense of fun, adventure, and daring, was even amplified by the deepening rut into which he found himself sinking. Bob, being Bob, decided it was time to change under his own terms.

Imagine my surprise and delight when he walked into the office one day and declared that he was quitting; he was selling his house and buying a yacht. It was now his intention to spend the rest of his life sailing round the world. Of course, we all showed our astonishment, some cheering their approval, others showing open contempt for his rashness.

Actually, nothing about this move had anything to do with rashness or quitting. Bob was no quitter.

He had known he was unhappy. He was aware that his current life was snuffing the spirit from him. He knew that, if he didn't take command of his situation, his situation would take command of him. He was being resilient, determined and organised for radical change.

No, this guy was not for quitting. To stay where he was would have been quitting!

In more detail, his plan was to sail around the world as many times as he could manage. He'd sail when the weather was favourable and stay put, wherever he was, when it was not. He'd live on the boat and work locally to earn cash flow for day-to-day costs. He invested his savings in long-term growth bonds to keep pace with inflation, or better, and set up long-term travel insurance (including health).

Eventually, if he ever became too ill or otherwise unfit to sail, he'd simply park up at a beach destination somewhere and cruise peacefully to his final port of call. He had shifted his plans from a single career destination, which he would never reach, to a completely serendipitous goal of tasting life. His plan became totally horizontal and he'd go where life led him. His goal was as open-ended as to live life.

At my last time of checking, he had sailed around the world at least four times and was still going strong. I raise my hat to him on every anniversary of that momentous day.

I would argue that non-linear plans are perfectly consistent with the concept of planning overall. Bob had a plan but it didn't fit any conventional model. It was in his heart for many years but he had never acted upon it. Eventually, life's curves brought him to a point where the unthinkable was not only thinkable, but preferable,

If our goal is to develop wisdom and insight, then a whole mix of life conditions and experiences can only add to it. If it is to become an expert in some field, then perhaps more direction and focus is required.

Navigating your own path

I'll leave it to you to decide, in terms of your own life, but there are some pretty common concepts you can use to help navigate the world and progress, in whichever way you decide: linear career, horizontal, vertical or non-linear, opportunistic.

1. Have clear goals

It really doesn't matter if our goals tend towards a linear career, a non-linear career or a combination of both. Nor does it matter if our progress is horizontal or vertical, or a combination of both. It does matter that we are clear about our ambitions and goals. It's important to recognise what's truly in our hearts and what will make our spirit soar.

Resilience and satisfaction will come only when we know we're doing something we want to be doing.

That's why having goals, and some kind of benchmark by which to track them, is so important. Too often we find ourselves stuck or dissatisfied in our lives, without knowing what the problem is. If we go back to our goals, we can check that what we're doing is truly meeting our aspirations.

2. Our lives are our own

Our heart's desires are exactly that - our heart's desires. There are lots of people in our lives and we hold a certain degree of responsibility to them.

Ultimately, however, this is our life and we get only one shot at each and every moment. If we compromise our dreams for others, it still needs to be on our own terms.

For example, many of my coaching clients tell me that having a family is a huge obligation, especially when the children are young. We want to nurture and guide them on the path to growing up straight and becoming good world citizens. When we are rearing those tender souls, I know that we want them to be guided by our deepest and most noble values.

Rearing them in our values is a fundamental reward to ourselves. Rearing children is not a liability or an encumbrance; it is a privilege and a joy if we let it be so.

More broadly, remember that every person in our lives is, first and foremost, the centre of their own lives. Or role is to guide, not to command, others. Our own life is the only one we can truly control and, in fact, we are the only ones who can control it.

Every compromise we make for others is our decision, and we should be doing it for our own advance. Service should be a privilege and not a trap.

3. Life is here and now

Just because we have some goals for the future, and a notional path to our destination, there is no need to suspend happiness, fulfilment and satisfaction in the present. Every day we put off happiness for 'jam tomorrow' is another day of draining our resilience and diminishing our existence.

We can think of our resilience as a kind of contingency fund.

Every day we are fulfilled and satisfied, we are adding *to* our fund of resilience. Every day we have to drag ourselves through, feeling dissatisfied and unfulfilled, we are drawing from our fund of resilience.

Too many days like that and our ability to deal with life's bumps and bends diminishes, our performance drops and stress levels climb. Being fulfilled today, and every day, builds resilience and fulfilment.

We'll need it for the tough times, when they come, so let's not drain it.

What's more, today - in fact now - is the only moment we can affect. The past has gone and the future hasn't or may never happen. We can have a reasonable expectation that the sun will rise tomorrow and we'll still be here, so it's sensible to have some sense of continuity and direction, beyond this moment, but that's no excuse to put off living right now.

Stop and check where you are, at this very minute. Of course, you're sitting somewhere comfortable and enjoying this book.

A good use of this moment.

But what's next? How is the rest of your day or week looking? Are you ready to fill it with the stuff that fulfils you?

Even the chores: are they a burden, or are they contributing to the quality and value of your life? Is work a joy? It may be routine but can you see that it is contributing to the bigger picture? Can you go to work with a smile on your face?

If the answer to any of these questions is 'no', it's time to stop and recalibrate what you're doing.

We have this moment only once. If we squander it, it will eventually impoverish us.

4. Smell the roses and savour the coffee

We often have our eyes so much on the far horizon, that we forget to sense the wealth of what we have all around us, now. We strive to do a good job and to reach a high value outcome... and then what?

We dive straight back into another task or challenge; we need to keep striving and driving along the path.

Next task, next milestone, next checkpoint.....

"Pretension is a poor joke that you play on yourself. Snap out of it. Recognise your strengths, work on your weaknesses. Real achievement is liking what you see in the mirror every morning."

Virat Kohli
Indian cricket captain

How often do we take time to review what we've done and to celebrate our achievements?

How many of us were brought up being told that it's a sin to be proud, boastful and full of our own successes?

It's true that nobody likes an overblown braggart. But there is a huge difference between recognising our worth, our achievements and successes, and being a show-off.

High fliers are very good at recognising their successes and drawing their own strength from them. They stop and congratulate others, and themselves, for a job well done. We can be sure that tough times will come along soon enough and it's great to have the confidence boost and the reminder that we can deliver value in challenging times.

When we are realistic about our real achievements and successes, we will be adding even more wealth to our resilience fund.

5. Diversions are not setbacks

Change is a fact of life. It's all around us, and it's not going anywhere, anytime soon.

Life (and partners or bosses) have ways of throwing us the odd curve ball. Even the most dedicated careerists get side-tracked from their primary goals and are forced to take an indirect path.

So how do we handle these diversions? This is where our non-linear goals really come into play.

Sure, it may take us a little longer to reach one of our direct goals, but let's make the most of it. What will we see and learn on this detour? Can we enjoy, and learn from, the detour in its own right?

How many times have we stumbled across a great new restaurant, or seen an old landmark from a different perspective, simply by taking a wrong turning? The universe has a neat way of challenging our perceptions and offering us a host of new opportunities. Diversions are always a matter of perspective and attachment to our plans.

'What's the big picture impact of this side track?' Maybe it's a minor inconvenience, or maybe it will fundamentally change our path and, perhaps, our overall goals. Maybe, just maybe, it's the universe's way of nudging us off the wrong path and onto the right one. Look at Bob's example, out of soul-sucking tedium, stepping into the light.

How many times have we been held up in traffic and late for an appointment? How many times has it really mattered? If it keeps on happening, perhaps it's time to reconsider our priorities. Do we give up more of our precious time to allow for delays and arrive exactly on time? Or are lives more important than the appointment? Are we living on the wrong side of town for the appointments we're trying to keep?

I live a lot of my life in Sydney, Australia. There is a running joke about 'Sydney time' where 15 minutes late is exactly on time.

I have friends who are perpetually late for social catch-ups and it drives my Scottish upbringing nuts! 'Laid back to the point of horizontal?', I moan. Yet it's not so in Sydney business. Fifteen minutes late and it's curtains: the interview is missed, the deal is cancelled, the moment is lost. So how come the same people can be so punctual in one arena and so lax in others?

There are always decisions we make, and adjustments we choose to make, or not, to fit the circumstances.

Whatever we choose, one thing is true. Getting stressed about it will simply diminish our resilience. Accepting, enjoying and learning from it will actually add to our reserves of resilience.

I have now come to appreciate my friends' tardiness. I factor it into my expectations and embrace their laid-back style. Fretting about it simply made me unhappy and put our relationships under stress. I'd go further: accepting their style has actually chipped away at my own Scottish Presbyterian punctiliousness and has brought me to a much more relaxed state. 'Go with the flow', I guess.

As for business, I feel nourished by its timeliness. It's all a matter of perception and context.

Then what happens with the big stuff? I'd say the same principles apply. If we lose our job, we may think it's the end of the world. Well, really, is it?

There will be a reason why it happened. It was either to do with our own personal performance or that of the company overall. Either way, it was a change waiting to happen. In a strange way, we might even consider it to be inevitable. After all, change is a constant.

The real question is not *'Why did it happen'* but rather *'How will I respond to this change. What can I do next?'*

I'm not a great believer in the phrase *'what doesn't kill us only makes us stronger'*. I see that as a way of compensating for, or even excusing, bad behaviour and actions.

In my view, everything makes us stronger if we are prepared to harvest the value that every waking moment offers us. Laid-back or timely, everything has its value.

Who knows, the diversion may actually show us the direction to totally different destination. Maybe the universe is trying to tell us something?

6. Constructive opportunism

None of us has total control of our destiny, but we are the only ones responsible for it.

We can lay down the most linear plan in the world, but we can only work with the opportunities that present themselves. That's where the opportunism element kicks in.

New opportunities come by, every day of our lives. The real art is to recognise them when they float past. The most successful, and famous, people are humble enough to recognise that some degree of chance, or good luck, plays a part in their success.

"Oftentimes I have been asked about the attributes for success, and I have said that you need two attributes for succeeding as an entrepreneur: one, courage, second, luck."

N. R. Narayana Murthy
I.T. Industrialist, Infosys Corp.

Even when we're totally happy where we are today, the 'next big thing' may come along, before we expect it.

Whenever one crops up, it's good to give new opportunities a close examination. It costs nothing to look.

If it feels right to move, hop aboard. If not, simply hold back, enjoy what you're doing and wait for the next opportunity to come along.

Of course, we can always cause more opportunities to come our way. We've all heard about being in the right place at the right time.

Sometimes it truly is a matter of circumstance, but we can certainly improve our chances of gaining opportunities.

By living in the mainstream, we can make sure that, if anything is on the move, we increase our chance of encountering it. Networking, seeking advice from others, showing interest in new and exciting things - these are all ways to have opportunities arise.

We can help fate along, if we are in the right place at the right time as often as possible, and we make it a matter of choice - very few new opportunities sail past our sofas.

Sitting at home with a bowl of chips balanced on our bellies is hardly going to widen our horizons, or introduce us to that one person.

We can always help ourselves by getting out there.

Finally, let's not forget that, sometimes, the most exciting opportunity can come out of left field. The chance encounter, the quirky suggestion, a moment of inspiration can lead to greatness.

So, keeping our eyes and ears open and letting opportunities present themselves will widen our opportunities and choices, as we let our hearts and minds be open, in what might be termed 'constructive opportunism'.

7. Living our purpose

Our life's purpose is about its quality of life, not its quantity or destination. Our purpose is more about why we were put on this earth, not about what we can accumulate while here. After all, we can't take it with us. Even our life's goals are a sub-set of our purpose.

I spend much of my time with clients exploring this very question. *'What is my life's purpose?'* I'm regularly surprised how often people simply don't know, or haven't even asked themselves the question.

Oddly enough, it turns out, on every occasion, that they do know their purpose; or at least their intuition does. It's simply that they haven't listened to their gut, or have dismissed the notion as fanciful.

Just as frequently, I see those same clients living a life that is unfulfilling, boring and even life-threatening. They are working away at goals and actions that simply don't match their purpose.

I urge every person I meet, and also you, my lovely readers, to step back, listen to your intuition, and get clear about life's purpose. It's amazing how all of the other issues in life simply recede and how easy it then becomes to make new and exciting decisions.

'So what', if we let a diversion take us on a different path with new destinations?

Our goals are a forecast, based on what we can see from here.

Our purpose is viewed from higher ground and gives a broader view.

Understand it and the goals become validated. Tasks fall into context and priorities become as simple as 1, ,2, 3.

Ignore our purpose and it's like feeling our way in the dark.

As we move forward and situations change, nothing is preventing us from reconsidering the big picture. Even our purpose can shift. It's important to take time regularly to review your goals and destination.

There's no need to be a rigid slave to 'the plan'.

Remember to download your free

Resilience

Workbook

Just follow the link below.

http://mikegordonbooks.com/download-sig-workbook/

You'll need the password that you find, at the end of Chapter 12

CHAPTER 3: TRUST AND MUTUAL RESPECT

> "No one who achieves success does so without acknowledging the help of others. The wise and confident acknowledge this help with gratitude."
>
> - Alfred North
> Whitehead, Mathematician, Philosopher

Compare the sentiments of the world's most successful entrepreneurs and leaders with those of many middle managers and supervisors. Contrast the opinions of those who have 'made it' and those who aspire to make it. Most successful people would agree that their success has been a result of vision, hard work and the help of others at key points along the way.

So why do so many of us try to go it alone, fear the collaboration of others and try to make it at the expense of those around us?

Can we make it to the top of our game or sustain a long and prosperous life, without the active support of others?

Can we develop resilience in life and thrive without the trust and mutual respect of others?

"Get respect for what you do and at the same time give it."

Estelle Parsons
Actress

I'd suggest that our success in life requires the support and participation of others in our lives. I believe that this acceptance, or rejection, of support reflects the difference we see between long-term vision and short-term fear.

Perhaps it's time to consider how we involve others in our lives as deliberate contributors, rather than seeing others as a source of interference, interruptions and disruption.

It's a cliché to say that we all live in a busy and crowded world, but being a cliché makes it no less true. Life is full of opportunity and adversity that confronts us on a daily basis. It's easy to become bamboozled by the choices and decisions we're asked to make, from one minute to the next. *'Should I do this, or that? Should I change it or leave it alone? Shall I stay or go? Should I suck it up or should I quit?'*

It's not surprising that more than 80 per cent of modern urbanites complain of stress and fatigue. With so many challenges all around us, trying to go it alone is simply exhausting.

In the hurly-burly of this life, let's stop and take pause.

Let's ask ourselves *'Do I behave like the leader of my own life, or like the manager of the tasks and demands that surround me? Which would I rather be?'*

Perhaps the answer is a little of each and our own behaviour will determine the kind of support that we get.

Leaders can lead, because others choose to follow them. Managers drive activities and meet goals, targets and deadlines. Getting things done usually needs a skilful balance of leadership vision and managerial controls. It'll often require the involvement and co-operation of others.

Forcing compliance from others turns us into dictators, not leaders. Mercilessly driving their labours turns us into tyrants, not managers. So let's be mindful of how we include the people we need and want to involve. Buy-in to our plans will be easier when people understand and agree with what we're trying to do. Collaboration and co-operation stem from good leadership, supported by clear and sensible management.

Trust and respect creates rapport and reciprocation with others in our lives. Those, in turn, are sure ways to build personal integrity and inner resilience in ourselves. In short, trusting others is a great way to achieve our own goals and strengthen our own abilities to deal with life along the way.

If it's true that we need the support of others in our lives and careers, then it'll be equally true that we need to develop a culture of trust and mutual respect around ourselves. What's more, respect is a two-way street. The respect we receive from others will be proportional, in large degree, to the respect we show towards them. Respect breeds respect; resentment breeds resentment.

I know that trust is hard to give to others: trust in their good faith; trust that they'll do the right things and trust that they'll do things right. Yes, all of those concerns are perfectly normal, and you're not alone in wrestling with the idea of giving trust to others. But look at the emphasis on 'them' in all of those concerns. How do we engender their trustworthiness?

Simple. By showing trustworthiness in ourselves. Trust is an inside-out energy, not an outside-in phenomenon.

It may take a huge cultural shift in us to embrace trust and respect with others. We may be the ultimate control freak who needs to micro-manage every single detail.

We may consider ourselves to be a very secret person and openly sharing ourselves doesn't come easily. We may have been stung in the past; let down or even swindled. Again, these are all perfectly normal reactions but, in today's world, they're not particularly helpful. Stress, fatigue and breakdown simply aren't practical and going it alone won't get us where we want to be.

No, our best option is to recognise that we need to trust other people to be involved in our lives and that we need to manage their inclusion carefully. And that will require us to be trustworthy towards them. Remember the adage: respect breeds respect; resentment breeds resentment. Let's turn the question on its head from *'should we trust others?'* to *'how can we trust others?' Ask yourself 'How can I ensure that I share trust and mutual respect with those who will help develop my life's ambitions?'*

Even if it's nerve-wracking, what's your alternative?

The rest of this chapter lays out some tried and tested methods for building trust, respect and co-operation with others and keeping it safe to do so.

Recognise our limitations

Life is hectic and increasingly complex. We simply can't know it all or do it all. Let's truly understand, and accept, that we will need help and support. It might be specialist knowledge, or skills we don't possess; or it may be that our capacity and effort are limited and we simply can't get it all done by ourselves.

Once we recognise our limitations, it becomes much easier to let go a little and reach out. It allows us to acknowledge the contributions others can make and to show gratitude for that help.

Magically, we're being more open and honest, showing a little of our vulnerability and beginning to build co-operation.

That's the open door through which trust and respect can enter.

Let's think about our 'resilience fund' (that we discussed in Chapter two) for a moment.

By drawing upon our resilience, opening up and trusting our team in that first instance, we signal our intention to work and communicate more effectively with others.

When we can be open and honest in our thoughts, and follow that through in our actions, we'll find we don't waste time and energy watching our backs. Showing our vulnerability to the right people will actually safeguard us against malice and sabotage by having others watch our back. Mutual trust and respect will form the foundation for long-term collaboration that gets things done.

In the end, those shared achievements will begin making huge investment deposits into our own resilience fund and we'll be net winners. We'll learn how to take on bigger and bigger challenges and involve others in turning the world into a better place. Now, at last, we'll begin to live on 'purpose' and our resilience will go stratospheric.

Honesty is best

You'll see that I've introduced the idea of honesty into the equation. Over the long term, duplicity and deceit will be unmasked and dishonesty will be uncovered. At that point, dishonest people will fall from grace and be excluded or abandoned. Honest people maintain respect towards themselves, even if they make a mistake. An honest mistake is manageable, and forgivable, a dishonest one brings mistrust and retaliation.

It's not naive to believe in the truth, or to develop a reputation for straight talking. Indeed, this kind of respect endears us to the very highest and most powerful people in our lives. Our loved ones, and our 'bosses' in life, rely on our honesty to keep them on the right path. 'Yes men' who peddle convenient truths, may be exploited in the short term but they will fail to thrive in the long term.

Honesty and transparency are the best approaches when involving others.

Once people know where they stand, they will have the choice to opt in or out. If they're in, they're in. If they're out, at least we know where we stand.

If we trick them into involvement, they'll probably catch on soon enough and will most likely leave us high and dry. Certainly, there's little chance of them staying over the long haul.

Be diverse

I'd also add diversity to the mix. Everyone is unique and might come from a different background and upbringing. They might hold different values from us and want to do things differently.

So let's learn to value and respect their uniqueness. After all, a great team has different individuals playing in different positions on the field.

"From each according to his abilities, to each according to his needs."

Karl Marx
Philosopher, economist, sociologist, journalist

Ideas can come from anywhere. When our family, friends and colleagues offer different opinions from ours, let's take the time to consider what they have to say and factor their insights into our decision-making.

After all, we don't have a monopoly on good ideas and approaches, do we?

Diversity of insight and approach invariably lead to more complete solutions, and will pay dividends when embraced positively. I'd go further and say that we can actively choose to seek out, and understand, the diverse values, different approaches and unique experience of others. It's not a case of *'They're wrong and I'm right'*; it's simply that they're different.

Leaders understand that others' upbringing may bring social and professional differences of behaviour and/or priorities. Over time, mutual respect will bring people together in a blended cultural norm for the whole team.

Teamwork wins

In my consulting life, we were always working in blended teams of total strangers. We'd go through a deliberate process we called 'Forming, norming, storming, performing'.

'Forming' was a phase of coming together and sharing something of ourselves with the team. 'Norming' was the active development of shared principles and practices that laid out preferences and expectations across the group. 'Storming' was getting action under way and 'Performing' was getting stuff done.

While, in business, this can become a structured team-building process, I'd suggest that every successful collaboration will go through those same steps before it becomes really functional.

There's nothing stopping us taking the same steps in our family and social lives to build that understanding, trust and rapport, right from the get-go.

The unique team culture that comes from this 'norming' process provides a sustainable differentiation that can't be copied.

The power of a blended team will always outstrip the performance of a team of clones. Ultimately you will all be able to say *'This is the way we do things around here'*, and productivity or achievements will soar.

Mindful communication

In families, social groups and work teams, we are communicating all day, every day. Whether we're sending emails and instant messages, or speaking face to face, it's communicate, communicate, communicate. It really helps when what we say is well received and understood.

When we are mindful of what we say, our message becomes purer in its intent and delivery. The better and more effectively we communicate, the richer our relationships become and the stronger the bond becomes. So let's be mindful and take responsibility for our words and actions. Are we speaking because we have something to share, that's of value to the audience, or simply to hear our own voices? That's the difference between something they need to hear, rather than something I need to say.

Clarity, simplicity and purity of message will always win over verbosity, venting and bluster. There is a huge impact in positive attitudes and speaking positively, especially to, or about, the people with whom we're collaborating. It might take another shift in attitude, but we can all learn the habit of speaking positively to others and providing quality feedback about the people we're working with.

Gossip is deadly and it can kill reputations in a heartbeat. Simply don't contribute to it. It's far better to build a reputation of trust and respect, by shining the best light on every situation, even when things don't go quite as planned.

The information we share (whether positive or negative) usually gets back to the person being discussed.

"Wise men speak because they have something to say; fools because they have to say something."

Plato
Philosopher

If we don't let negative emotions impact the people around us, they will return our good intention with their own good will. People enjoy hearing that we've said supportive things about them and will know that we are on their side. That will build trust and actually deliver free deposits into our resilience fund, without us even knowing.

Manners matter

The old adage says 'Manners cost nothing' but not having them could cost us everything.

In a busy world small gestures of kindness go a long, long way. It takes scarcely any effort to take those extra seconds to say 'thank you' or to acknowledge other people's efforts; but just watch their faces light up when we do.

Even if things aren't quite right, make the effort to deliver feedback and suggestions kindly.

This includes everyone from the cleaner to the big boss; from the youngest to the oldest.

"Good manners are appreciated as much as bad manners are abhorred."

Bryant H. McGill
Human rights author, activist

How would it feel to be famous for being even-handed, helpful and kind? It's so much better than the opposite. Remember that a good reputation helps to make us resilient and to take ever bigger steps towards our purpose. A simple 'thank you' is a tiny step closer to our heart's desire.

And let's be kind. Yes, be kind. I know it's an old-fashioned notion, but human nature doesn't rely on being trendy. It's been honed over millennia and it's how it is, because it works. Listen when people are speaking; ask questions out of genuine interest; wait for others to catch up with the key points of a discussion.

These actions show respect and will encourage others to help us when we don't quite get it – and there will be times when we don't quite 'get it' and need the help. I like to think of manners and kindness as the lubricants that keep our team's machine well-oiled and running smoothly.

I hope that all this talk about trust, honesty and respect doesn't sound like mere abstract ideals, like some spiritual dogma or other. They're truly not and I'm sharing them as hard and tangible practices.

They're real things made up of real words and actions. And they have a flow between each of the players. What's more, trust and respect flow best in a spirit of sharing, as equals, across the board.

Sharing ourselves

Sharing begins with ourselves, so let's share more of who and what we are. One of the best ways to build respect is to let others know what's driving our aims. This can come by sharing our dreams and vision, our knowledge and our personality. Let people get to know us and like us.

They'll want to hear more from us and they will find us more approachable. Magically, more solid relationships will begin to grow.

If ever I feel fearful to share myself, all I do is simply think, ahead of time, about what I want to say and be more prepared. That preparation and clarity demonstrates my respect for those I meet and they'll reward me with attention and closer involvement.

Of course, there is the scope for people to abuse our openness, but we've already taken the time to choose our team carefully, so the risks are minimised. I recommend that we be bold and open ourselves up some more.

Sharing what we know can also feel risky. The age-old maxim that 'information is power' might have been true in the past, but it omits to add that power used unwisely is tyranny.

In the new world of shared goals and team-based participation, withheld information acts as a drag on trust and productivity.

Information is a common resource that will propel the whole team forward, be that at work, at home or socially. Of course there will always be questions of confidentiality, but this brings us straight back to the question of trust.

Shared goals and common purpose are much stronger for our overall security than a combination lock on our hearts or a zipper on our lips. When we trust our partners we liberate their thinking and help them to achieve the best outcomes for the team and ourselves.

> ### "We are not cisterns made for hoarding; we are channels made for sharing."

Billy Graham
Evangelist

While we're about it, let's make our sharing purposeful. I fear for the Facebook and Twitter generation. So much is out there and can never be taken back. What seemed cool to share with our buddies at 14, might come back to haunt us in later life and in different contexts.

I'm not advocating a total open season on our lives and knowledge. If shared knowledge is a differentiator, let's not squander it in the public domain.

Empathy, not sympathy

That's where trust and respect play an important part. Choosing our partners, and being mindful of what we share, will always remain our own responsibility. There is a balance and judgment to be struck about how much to share, with whom and when.

Is there a difference between empathy and sympathy? Of course there is and empathy will win out every time.

A sympathetic *'there, there, there.'* may make us feel like we've done our bit for team sharing, but it's not very helpful to the recipient.

It's OK to let people know that we understand how they feel when things are going well, and when they're not. It's truly helpful to go beyond merely recognising how things are tracking to acknowledging the personal impact that success or mishaps bring to all of us.

Celebrate the joys for everyone's sake, not just because we've got some benefit out of it personally. When things go awry, put ourselves in other people's shoes instead of immediately assuming that they are wrong and we are right.

By sharing the joys together and holding joint accountability for the shortfalls, the team gets stronger, motivation grows and efforts are redoubled. And who benefits in the long run? We do, of course. Our goals get met more readily and we draw even closer to our purpose. Our resilience fund gets yet another boost.

Get involved

Finally, seek to get involved and don't be afraid to ask others for help. Get involved in mutual projects and activities that serve other people's goals, as well as exclusively your own.

The more we can participate together, across the board, the better we get to know each other. We inevitably end up enjoying working with each other and getting more things done together. We form closer connections because we are working directly with each other to meet shared goals. We will appreciate each other's support and get to know each other better.

Participation quickly turns into collaboration and the best outcomes flow for everyone.

As you can see, there is no single 'silver bullet' to creating and maintaining an environment of trust and mutual respect. Equally, it's true that, without trust and mutual respect, our plans will probably stall in the medium term, and fail in the long term.

So, one of the best ways to side-step those agonising moments of *'Should I quit?'* is to get connected.

Start sharing and build trust throughout our networks. Tasks get shared around, effort becomes spread more evenly and results simply get better. Through all of this, our lives become smoother and happier and our resilience fund is filled more and more.

I've highlighted just some of the ways that we can help develop respect and trust in our lives. However, these can only be successful if our intent is based upon our own trust and respect.

Developing trust and respect certainly requires a positive frame of mind for collaboration but, even more importantly, it requires heart. We need to be ready to embrace trust and respect with others, at our very core.

It can't simply be a question of grudging acceptance or need, nor an intellectual mechanism to enlist support. I can't emphasise strongly enough that it needs to be genuine and authentic. Collaboration is a way of life, not painted on for effect.

So let's be brave. Let's embrace collaboration and build a team we can trust and respect with confidence. Our goals will fall into place more easily and our ability to thrive through difficult moments will grow and grow.

Remember to download your free

Resilience

Workbook

Just follow the link below.

http://mikegordonbooks.com/download-siq-workbook/

You'll need the password that you find, at the end of Chapter 12

CHAPTER 4: WHAT'S IT WORTH?

"When wealth is lost, nothing is lost; when health is lost, something is lost; when character is lost, all is lost."

Billy Graham,
Evangelist

Value, like beauty, is in the eye of the beholder.

It doesn't matter if we're talking about our careers or the day-to-day tasks of everyday life, we work for a reason -- but how often do we forget why we are doing what we are doing? Whether it's paid work, or unpaid, we find ourselves living to work, rather than working to live.

How often do we end the day asking ourselves *'Is this really worth it?'*

By then, we've probably slipped into a pattern where we're so caught up in the 'whats' and 'hows' of life that we begin to forget about the 'whys'.

Why are we doing what we're doing disappears into the minutia of what we are doing; stressing about the *'How will I get this done?'* rather than *'why am I doing this?'*.

That's when the uneasiness and doubts begin to creep in and we ask: *'Should I quit?'*.

By the time we've reached that point, it's already getting to an end-game for whatever we're doing. We've lost sight of the prize, the frustration has mounted and the tasks in front of us seem unsurmountable.

And you know what I'm going to say, don't you? Yes. It's time to step back and review the situation. It's time to step away from the detail and remember the 'why' of what we're doing.

In this chapter, we'll explore what value is and what it means for us. We'll look at the rewards we're seeking and getting and the effort (the cost) of getting it.

Of course, the real outcome is to decide whether the input cost is worth the outcome we're actually getting.

So let's begin with the whole question of value.

What does value mean to each of us? If we're smart about it, we'll recognise that our notion of value is completely unique to each of us and we each have our own yardstick of success.

Yet, too often, the simplest answer we come up with is one that centres around money, in some shape or form.

Over the decades since World War II, we've allowed ourselves to slip into an economy-based view of the world, rather than a society-based one.

Typically, we offer our labour and creativity in return for money and benefits (usually also described in monetary terms).

We express value in some kind of economic terms.

'I go to work to earn money to put my kids through school. Their education will give them a better start in life and get them a better job'.

Too often we lose the connection of education to quality of life, and instead opt for quantity.

"The love of family, and the admiration of friends, is much more important than wealth and privilege."

Charles Kuralt
Journalist, broadcaster, author

Even if we're a stay at home mum and work for no direct pay, we will still think of our contribution in terms of providing a clean and safe place for the rest of the family to go out and earn or study. In short, we put our labours in for indirect financial gain.

An exquisite twist, on the unpaid homemakers, is the case of the mums who go out to work to earn enough money to send their kids to pre-school or kindergarten. The financial gain is often zero, but they justify their life disruption in terms of giving the kids a 'better start'.

Really? A better start to what? They'd say a better start at elementary school. Why? In order to get to a better high school, college and job. Even at 18 months old, kids are being channelled into the cult of money before living.

Then there's the small business owner. We often set up a business because we want to be our own boss. Or perhaps we have a particular skill that we've turned into a livelihood. These individuals are probably my toughest clients. They've become so absorbed in running the business, and dealing with its many demands, that a personal life has been sacrificed almost entirely.

First there's running the front of house with the clients. Then there's the back office of stock ordering, accounts, websites and advertising, payroll and all of the other pieces needed to keep the business running.

Finally, there are the regulatory requirements - health and safety, insurances, monthly or quarterly reporting and tax. Most often I find that these clients have spent all day at 'work' then bring home a whole case of 'admin' to do in the evenings. In the final analysis, they dare not calculate their actual rate of pay. If they divide their take home earnings by the number of hours at work and administration, they'd probably find that they're earning well less than the minimum wage - all for the liberty of being their own boss.

In short, they end up more married to the business than they do to their family. That's definitely time for a review of values.

What's worse, we begin to use the 'money yardstick' as a way of comparing our success with others. We bring everything down to the lowest common denominators of money and things. Stuff before substance. If we can't apply a number or a brand to what we do, it soon loses its value. Now don't get me wrong, money is important; we all need to pay the bills and put food on the table at home. But let's not run away with the idea that it's the end of the story.

We spend increasingly more hours of our week at paid or unpaid work and it is consuming our lives more and more - long hours, long distances, high workload and narrowing focus. Of course, there are more and more demands on us, to do even more of this. But there is a tipping point somewhere along the line. At some stage, our living output begins to exceed our life rewards. No wonder we end up living to work, rather than the opposite.

We then burden it with pseudo-social or moral overtones like the Protestant 'work ethic' or the Catholic 'to work is to pray' or even 'dig for the country'. Each of these is merely an external notion of value, which we hear from our earliest years. Look around and hear what we say to each other. These ideas are all around us.

Like all external views of ourselves, they are inaccurate and misdirecting. So it's no wonder that we forget to ask ourselves the question 'Why?' Eventually the external justifications wear thin and our need for authenticity develops.

Surely there's got to be more reward in our lives than simple dollars and cents, or duty. Isn't it now time to think back to the bigger picture and regain our sense of true value; our sense of self and our purpose?

If we go to a paid job, we can ask ourselves some searching questions about what we really value at work. Consider:

- Do I want a job that is simply high-paying?

- What will I do with the money?

- How much time, effort, heart and soul am I spending there?

- Will I have time to enjoy the fruits of my labour?

Have you noticed that all of these questions have centred around the 'what's' of the job and being at work. We've silently accepted the notion of needing to go to work without considering the purpose.

Maybe it's time to add the softer side of value at work:

- Are we seeking a job that gets respect from others?

- Do we want a job that allows us to help others in some way?

- Is it important to gain new skills, pick up knowledge, learn?

- Can we balance our time with our family and friends and do the activities we enjoy?

- Do we need to use our brains in solving problems and be challenged mentally at work?

- Do we like to be in charge, have people come to us for advice?

- Do we enjoy making decisions, or is that too risky for our peace of mind?

Of course, there is no simple answer to these questions and one response will not fit all. Our mix of answers, and even the importance of each question, will be unique to each of us.

Getting value from our work starts with us - our needs and desires. Let's be clear about what we want and, by adding some of these softer issues, we can begin to tell if we're living our purpose, or not.

"If you do a job you love, you'll never work a day in your life"

Albert Einstein
Philosopher and Scientist

Try saying the following sentence to yourself. Say it aloud, if you can.

'I am at the centre of my world.'

How comfortable did that feel?

I meet many, many clients who are living their lives at the 'service' of others. Parents and spouses are particularly good at this. Being able to be of service to others is a fantastic gift for which we can be truly grateful. But it's a delicious trap.

The 'feel good' sucks us in and we soon strive for more and more of it. Before long, our every waking hour becomes focused on other people's needs. We begin to disappear from the priorities and, soon, we vanish completely from the equation. Guess what happens next?

Yep, that's right, we get lost and begin to ask *'Should I quit?'*

Be in no doubt, our work, careers or 'service to others' is entirely our business. What we make of it begins and ends with us. So, let's get our mind-set right and get value, for ourselves, from what we do.

I had a client recently, Liz, who felt trapped by her sense of service and duty, exactly like this. She was a wife and mother and the primary homemaker. She had a part-time job, four mornings a week. On top of that, she was supporting her two elderly parents across town. She was stretched beyond capacity.

Why did she put herself under such strain? Her answer was: *'Because they need me and I love them. Besides, there's nobody else to do it'.*

It took a few months of unravelling this set of beliefs in Liz, to get some 'Liz Life' back. But we got there. By the end, Liz was happier, felt more in command of her life and was even having a social life.

It started with the kids. No more domestic slave. If they wanted clean clothes, they would share in laundry duties. Meals were cooked on a roster agreed between husband and older kids. Housework was a shared responsibility. If one of the family shirked it, then the job simply didn't get done. Peer pressure would eventually get the task completed. And the same with the husband and the parents - life logistics became a shared operation and Liz began to get some free time back to herself.

Of course, the two biggest objections from Liz were guilt (*'I'm such a bad mother/wife/daughter'*) and doubt (*'They're useless. They'll never be able to do it'*). Guess what. Once we got the prize in sight, a happy and de-stressed Liz (the mum, wife, daughter) emerged and all those objections simply melted. The 'why' over-rode any of the 'what' or 'how' obstacles.

We can all be like Liz. We can put ourselves at the centre of our own worlds, and co-ordinate all of the satellites that orbit around us into a beautiful universe.

Let's start by valuing ourselves. If we don't develop a strong respect for ourselves, we can't really expect others to do it for us.

Of course, we often find it very difficult to value ourselves. It really goes against the grain to do so.

How many of us were brought up in a way where giving was encouraged and receiving was considered to be almost a sin? Where recognising others was good, but recognising our own achievements was vanity? Yet our external environment becomes a reflection of what is inside us. Take ourselves seriously and others will, too: don't... and they won't, either.

We can only get value when we begin to value ourselves. Our sense of purpose will guide us to know what's best for ourselves and the world will begin to manifest it around us. If we centre our sense of value around others, everyone else prospers while we become the drudge.

For those of us that have ever flown, let's remember the aircraft flight safety instructions about the little yellow oxygen masks. We're told to put on our own mask first before helping others. Why is this? Simple; you're absolutely useless to anyone else if you're dead. In fact, your dead body will probably block the way for others trying to escape.

Now that's a bit graphic, I grant you, but the essence of the message is true. If we spend all our time for the benefit of others, and forget about our own wellbeing, we'll end up burned out and without value to them. Our best strategy is to be fit and well enough to be of service for the good of everyone -- and that begins with ourselves.

If you're looking for a daily mantra, or just a catch-phrase, to start each day, try this:

Self-nurture is not selfish. My best self is the greatest gift I can give to others.

In fact, self-nurture is only the beginning of our life's value chain.

We also need to be able to engage, communicate and work with others. Criticism is all around us and our resilience to it starts from within. Do we hold, and remember, our sense of self-worth in those situations? Irrespective of whether we receive praise or criticism, let's not be seduced, or even deflected by it.

Our sense of value, and measures of success, really depend on what we think about ourselves. Our own good intentions are the best guide to 'success'. If we base our whole identity on what others think about us, we'll probably end up nowhere, bouncing from one opinion to another, being considered indecisive and passed over. Keeping a realistic view of our own contribution will help us thrive and, at the same time, get value for us.

Often, our own unique perspective will highlight things that don't feel right and could be made better. How often do we hold back from expressing ourselves? How desperate are we to fit in? Though it is important to follow certain rules, we really shouldn't hesitate to express our thoughts and intuitions. If we don't know or understand something, ask. If we spot an inefficiency or creaky process, call it out. If we can see a way to make all of our lives better, don't hold back?

Certainly some of our bosses or colleagues (at work or in life) may see suggestions as criticism or interference, so we do need to handle our views carefully. But really, do we want to live in an environment of silent obedience and total compliance to the status quo? Balanced communication is the key here. Being engaged will bring us greater value from what we are doing and an effective communication pattern will deliver greater success than we'd get without it.

Remember our discussion in chapter three, and simply 'be kind'.

All of this discussion of our value and worth doesn't mean, however, that we're talking about a free ride. It's important to pay the ticket price. We always need to be very clear that our contributions are genuine and sincere, from within us, and of value to others, as they perceive value.

Good quality work that fits the bill is a fundamental requirement, which gets us basic rewards. High reward will only come by delivering above the basic levels expected of us. To get value, we need to provide it. We can't expect to receive the glittering awards for slacking the whole day and we do need to do our best to play within the rules.

Look around. If we're already valuing ourselves and expressing it kindly, chances are everyone else will probably see it too. They probably value us already.

Too often we are our own worst enemy; our own worst critic or our own worst task master. It's healthy to be realistic about what a good job, well done, looks like. Being unrealistic about reality, by being too hard on ourselves, is counter-productive, diminishing and drains our resilience. A good outcome deserves acknowledgment so we should accept praise or gratitude with grace.

Why diminish praise when we deliver 'merely' a good job, rather than perfection? Whose measure of success is at play here? Is it realistic to reject praise in favour of our own higher standard?

Too often, in our own minds, we keep ourselves busy striving for absolute perfection and always falling short. We're the ones who are blind to success, because of our own unrealistic standards and expectations. Making the shift to realistic self-respect and valuing our real achievements is exactly the behaviour that will help us to feel success. And I emphasise the word 'realistic'.

Remember, a Rolls-Royce and a Skoda are both quality cars. Quality is about meeting the required standards. Obviously the standards of each car are very different in terms of performance, features and luxury, but both do the job they are required to do. They meet their own specifications.

Are we seeking to deliver a Rolls-Royce when a Skoda will do the job adequately in most everyday situations? Equally, we'd object to paying a Rolls-Royce price tag and be delivered a Skoda in return. Mutual balance is the essence of fairness.

Simply accept that people around us have always been seeing our value, even if we've been downgrading it under the lens of perfection.

When we work towards valuing the person we are, and respecting the job we've done, we will arrive at a better mind-set to our actions, we'll create success for ourselves and we'll get value from what we do. So will others.

By this point we've defined some parameters of value for ourselves and we've got our heads in the right place. Now we need to make sure that the value starts to flow and keeps on coming. It won't do so unless we take active steps to let it flow.

When we want to achieve success, or failure, we should be ready to take responsibility. If doing the bare minimum, and going home at five every day are our goals, then stepping up the pace may not be the answer.

Money, jobs and career are great ambitions to have, if that's what we want. But why do we want them? These are enablers to success, not success in themselves. So, what will money bring us? What will a growing career add to our life overall? Only when we're clear about those answers will we be in a position to concentrate our efforts.

Every day Steve Jobs would ask himself

"If today were the last day of my life, would I want to do what I'm about to do today?"

Steve Jobs
Founder, Apple Corporation

Sadly, in the end, he voiced a fundamental regret:

"I wanted my kids to know me. I wasn't always there for them, and I wanted them to know why and to understand what I did."

Steve Jobs
From an 'open letter' published posthumously

Is more less?

It's tempting to want to move up the success ladder, because that's what we've been raised to want and expect, but is it right for us individually?

Remember, to get value from our work will depend largely upon our own sense of what value is.

Was Steve Jobs' payment the right cost for what he got out of life?

When we look back over the careers of successful people, we learn that they usually end up in a very different job or different career path from the one that they set out on. Circumstances have an odd way of taking over, and we can lose sight of what we're all about. Having a plan is great, but plans change. Live with it.

Change can be forced upon us, or new opportunities can lead us to change direction. We need to be prepared for change and stay ahead of the curve.

Change happens

I'm always intrigued when clients are surprised by, or fearful of, change. We are among the most adaptable animals in the world. There isn't a continent, environment or situation in which human beings don't thrive.

We are inherently resilient, creative and adaptable. We can live with anything that the universe throws at us. Change is a fact of life. It's part of our path, not a diversion. It's a way of living.

Flexibility in our plans will take us a long way if we're ready to roll with the changes. We should always be asking: *Is this a good change? How will this allow the value I want to keep flowing?*

Negotiate change

There's always a new deal to be struck with the world. If it's a 'yes' to this change, we can go with it as it comes. If not, is there a better alternative? Or, even, are we better off staying put and weathering the storm until a better day comes along? Ignoring a change certainly won't help and may even cut the flow of life's value short.

When change comes, everything becomes a negotiation - accept, change, reject. So what 'win' will this change bring us? Every deal has a win-win, or it's not a deal at all. If we win when someone else loses, we've become an exploiter, and our own worth diminishes. If they win and we lose, we've become a victim and our own worth diminishes. When we both win, hey, we both win! Our immediate payback is positive, our self-esteem is enhanced and our reputation grows. Win-wins do exist in every deal, or it's not a deal at all.

We should never be afraid to walk away from deals that just don't come together.

Every deal has a 'walk away' price, at the point where the cost outweighs the benefit - a better alternative to a negotiated agreement.

By understanding what we really value, our 'walk away' becomes clear and we can negotiate with confidence.

When we're willing to walk away, we'll usually be pleasantly surprised at how much better our negotiations turn out. Suddenly, what we offer carries value and the tables turn in our favour.

Keep the value flowing by accepting only the right deals - right for us, and right for the other party, that is.

Distraction of the new

Then there's the question of 'shiny new things'. A bigger job title usually comes with a pay raise and more perks, but is that what we really want? Is the increased responsibility, time and effort it will take really worth it? Does the new job bring the right kind of value for us?

Just because other people are hightailing their way up the ladder, does not make that right for us.

At times like this, I like to use the 'plate in front of me' analogy.

Imagine we're in our favourite restaurant and we're ready to order. We've looked at the menu and we've selected exactly what we want to eat. We order it and it comes.

Now imagine that the guy at the table next to us stands up, and walks across to us, carrying his own plate. He tries to scrape the peas off his plate and onto ours. Do we accept the peas just because they're coming our way? How would we feel?

Too right! We'd be outraged. We didn't want peas. We didn't order them and we're certainly not going to accept them off someone else's plate. We'd stop him in his tracks.

Well, that's an example of what would have been an unacceptable deal. He wins, we lose. It's simply not a deal.

It may sound like a silly example but it's exactly what happens every day of our lives.

People try to engage us in ways we wouldn't choose and probably wouldn't want. Just because it's different, doesn't mean it's better.

They may offer inducements, rewards or even threats to encourage us to accept.

If the deal isn't right, don't take it.

Whose value?

At work, in our own business or at home, it's always a question about our sense of value. Our own motivation and success are held within us, not in a new job, new title or new responsibilities.

Value sits within our own definition. We need to take time to evaluate the full impact of any proposition and before we take on added responsibility. Once again, is it a price we're prepared to pay for the returns on offer?

That's where the big picture kicks in. We live in today's busy environment and we can get locked into a preoccupation with what's right in front of us; today's schedule, our 'to do' lists or other people's demands. Too often, we forget about how success might look for us, five years from now.

What if we write a brief personal vision statement, make a list, or draw a picture that sets out our most important values and the key parts of our lives?

We all know that we can't soar when we're lacklustre today: equally, forgetting about the future will drive us into a rut and we'll never soar then, either.

Urgent or important?

Even when we're engaged in a crisis, things will go much better, and value will keep flowing, when we keep our perspective of the shorter and longer terms. Just because things can be urgent doesn't mean that they're important. Our true value comes from focusing on what's important, not merely urgent or immediate.

And, while we're thinking about it, urgent to whom?

How often has someone run in, demanding that we take action 'right now'? It might be our boss at work, a client wanting a rush order or our child needing clean sports gear for school. We've already got our own day scoped out and it's got a certain rhythm to it. Now this!

Here's a great opportunity to step back and review the big picture. Review it with the 'urgent demander'. *'Why is this so urgent? What has brought this to a point of crisis? Why is it our responsibility to pull it out of the fire? What'll happen if it doesn't get done? Who else could do it?'*

Then there's the killer question: *'How could you let this happen?'*

That's right, you, not me.

Accountable or responsible?

Just think about it. How many crises have we created in our lives, or for other people? By comparison, how many are we expected to fix? Interesting balance, isn't it?

Think about the peas example. Who ordered peas they didn't want? Us? No. Someone else went off the rails and they want us to get them back on track. We have a choice - to help or not. That's a negotiation, right there and then.

There's a very common affliction, which hits many of my mentoring and small business clients. Not knowing when to stop.

When we've ended for the day, just stop! When we take our vacation, be on vacation! We need to develop the discipline to remove ourselves from the job completely.

One last bit of tidying up, while there's a spare moment, is not personal down-time. When the job's done, offering to check emails and voicemail while we are away is simply unhealthy.

Remember to stop

Whose anxiety are we serving by taking work away with us or not stopping? To keep the value balance positive, we need to know when to turn the tap off. The world will not collapse in a heap when we walk out the front door or sit down and have a cup of tea.

Back to the big picture, when is it really time to leave our current situation?

I'm absolutely not talking about quitting; I'm talking about embracing change on our terms. We should never be afraid to get off the boat, and there's a big difference between abandoning ship, and a planned disembarkation.

We can't live in fear of the next big change. When the value stops flowing, or slows down, it's time to review our options. We need to be flexible, when it comes to our overall career path, even if it means changing midway.

So let's keep value flowing at its optimum, by keeping ourselves in the right stream.

Although scary, change is sometimes necessary and can be very good for us.

This brings us right back to the question of our own resilience. We've talked about understanding our values and engaging with the world - knowing what we do, and don't, want and what we're prepared to exchange, to get that value. Living a full life and getting full value from it.

Stay in shape

Being that engaged with life needs energy and fortitude. It's time to get in shape.

Our success, and rewards, are directly influenced by everything we do to stay in shape – physically, mentally, emotionally and spiritually.

We need to manage our fitness and energy levels, as well as identifying the best time to do our best work. That way, we'll build the resilience that will keep us going, and maximise the value.

Every now and again I need to take a good look at myself.

- Have I become lethargic, sitting in front of my computer or TV? Time for a swim.

- Is my mind buzzing from too much thinking and internal debate? Time to meditate or go for a walk in the park.

- Is my client work becoming repetitive or routine? Time for some research and learning how to take it further.

- Is my writing boring even me? Time to step away from the keyboard and refresh.

- Am I questioning my every move? Time to reconnect with friends and family and get an outside perspective.

Yes, there are lots of things I do to stay in shape, mentally as much as physically. No one of them is a silver bullet.

There are different actions to hit specific targets, depending upon what going on. Collectively, however, they end up making me stronger, and more resilient, for whatever comes along.

Have you worked out your resilience building plan?

"Health is the greatest gift,
contentment the greatest wealth,
faithfulness the best relationship."

Buddha
Enlightenment teacher

So, in summary, getting value from our lives needs us to take responsibility for a few key factors

1. Know what value means to us.

2. Balance the cost of getting the value against the outcome and keep it positive.

3. Realising that change is a way of life.

4. Understanding that everything's a negotiation.

5. Accepting that walking away isn't quitting.

6. Keeping in shape via resilience and adaptability.

 Remember to download your free

Resilience

Workbook

Just follow the link below.

http://mikegordonbooks.com/download-siq-workbook/

You'll need the password that you find, at the end of Chapter 12

CHAPTER 5: GIVING VALUE

"The price of success is hard work, dedication to the job at hand, and the determination that, whether we win or lose, we have applied the best of ourselves to the task at hand."

Vince Lombardi
American football player, coach, executive

There are so many everyday sayings about getting something for nothing. One of the most common I hear is: 'There is no such thing as a free lunch.'

Basically it's saying that, if we want to gain something, we need to earn it or pay for it in some other way. If we want to advance, we're constantly reminded that we need to 'pay our dues'.

Less common are the ideas about getting value from free stuff -- 'What comes for free has no value.'

These ideas about valuing free stuff are a little more complex. This is about our own sense of understanding value. If it was easy to come by, then we tend to have little sense of attachment to it, or to see it as worth less.

Maybe 'easy come, easy go' is another expression of the principle of valuing something differently, through having to earn it for our own sake, not as a result of paying some kind of price or tax to others for getting it.

"All life demands struggle. Those who have everything given to them become lazy, selfish, and insensitive to the real values of life. The very striving and hard work that we so constantly try to avoid is the major building block in the person we are today."

Pope Paul VI

There's also the question of giving stuff for free. Is there ever really the concept of true altruism or pure generosity? We may tell ourselves that we're giving freely, but we might actually be giving for some kind of 'feel-good' in return.

Putting money into a charity box may actually be a complicated act of payback, for something that we have already been given. I've seen clients who feel the need to atone for their sense of guilt about having received, when they don't feel worthy. Is our 'gift' actually a subtle fee or commission?

Often our 'giving' is, in fact, an investment in a society which we'd prefer to live in.

When we give for the benefit of those we love, or respect, is it in the hope that we bond more closely, or that their wellbeing will benefit us in some way?

Then there's the flip-side to our giving - whether we realise it or not, we may actually be making the recipient more beholden, or indebted, to us. Is our 'gift' actually a subtle trap?

Finally, back to the question of free stuff having little value. How will our recipients value our 'gift'? Remember it has come to them 'for free', so their sense of attachment to it, or of its value, will be just as slight as ours might have been. It's probably unrealistic to expect that others will value our 'gift' more than we might have done ourselves.

I suggest that everything that is given, or received, is actually an exchange of value. It therefore works best when we have a sense of what the value is to each party.

As a recipient, we can demonstrate our gratitude and show our appreciation for what the gift means to us. As the giver, we can share our intention and be clear about why we are giving. It then allows us to accept appreciation and gratitude with clarity and genuine good will. Each gives and receives mutual value which is merely manifested in the thing that's being given.

Yes, altruism is a rare thing, if it ever really exists at all. Better, by far, to understand that every transaction is an exchange of mutual value, or else it's no deal at all.

At work, we 'give' our creativity and labour for money. In a shop, we 'give' our money for goods or services. At home, we might contribute housework chores, while someone else cooks the dinner or fixes the car.

In this chapter we'll explore the ideas of giving value to others. Regardless of where we look on the spectrum between pure altruism and a cash transaction, there is almost always an exchange of value.

It's rarely a one-way thing.

We can think of this chapter as the return flow of 'getting value', which we discussed in the previous chapter 'What's it worth?'

We'll also spend some extra time focusing on our work lives, simply because it's one of the most obvious examples of an exchange of value.

> "Far and away the best prize that life has to offer is the chance to work hard at work worth doing."
>
> Theodore Roosevelt
> US President, 1901-1909

We wouldn't expect to work for free in our day jobs; nor would we expect our employers to hand us fistfuls of money for doing nothing.

Bear in mind, however, that the concepts of giving value are true in all areas of our lives.

Building value, engaging with others and adding to our resilience involves some kind of value exchange, somewhere along the line. As we read this chapter, we can reflect and apply the concepts of giving value, whoever we are and whatever we're doing.

So let's get back to the most fundamental question, one we explored in the previous chapter: *What is value?*

This time, however, we'll look at what value means to those receiving it from us, rather than our sense of the value we expect to receive. Let's be clear what 'value' means to our recipients; either the person or the organisation.

Clarity counts

Sometimes expected value will be stated directly, as in a contract, a charter, an agreement or terms and conditions. It's easy to believe documents like those and we all too often kid ourselves that the terms in the document are all that's required. They're not.

For example, simply turning up for work may be the substance of the 'attendance' clause in the contract. It's unlikely to add the condition of '... *with a smile on your face*'. Yet we've all felt the expectations around a positive attitude to work, on top of the simple duration, or workload, conditions that were explicitly laid out. Tacit expectations run through any contract.

We started talking about giving value, as a means to get value in return. Well, doing our job may give us the money we wanted, but what about our other expectations? Prime positions, best quality jobs, bonuses, and even a positive working atmosphere, all depend upon perceived attitude.

Think about the 'spirit' of the agreement, not only the 'letter' of the document. Let's be aware of what are we actually signing up for, whether spoken or silent.

Sometimes, the value exchange remains completely tacit or silent; where we are all expected to understand what's expected, or at stake, without ever saying it out loud. Friends and family are very good at assuming that things are equal and balanced, when they agree to something.

How often have we traded jobs with a friend; one task for another? '*I'll tidy your yard if you fix my computer.*' I've had occasions where that kind of trade has worked very well for each party. I've also seen some complete disasters, where one side has actually made something worse for the other.

Most often, it just doesn't live up to expectations: incomplete, insufficiently thorough, poor quality, too long or too late in delivery.

I once fixed a friend's computer software upgrades while she cooked dinner. The upgrades were more complex than expected (of course!) but they eventually went in perfectly (of course!). Sadly, the dinner my friend cooked was totally inedible. It was awful!

We're (still) good friends and we've learned to laugh about it now; but it was touch and go for a while. She had assumed that software upgrades were easy things to complete and I had assumed that she knew how to cook. We both learned some new truths and, eventually, got the value. It's just wasn't the value that either of us expected.

As a starting point, we can all do the research and understand what is meant by value in another party's eyes. At work, it could be throughput in a process or revenue from sales, or even cost reduction. Whatever it is, we can learn about it, and begin to live it.

Then we can make sure that our activity is aligned to the organisation's, or individual's, principal goals. We can consider *'How does my personal activity contribute to their bottom line?'* And their expected value can take on many surprising forms - revenue up; costs down, quicker output, better quality. Even at home, it may be as vague as a social night out, with my 'happy side' showing.

What should we do, if we can't research the answer in books or on the internet? Simple: Just ask! That's right, a few minutes of clarification can go a long way towards understanding expectations.

Once we're clear, we can spell out what we understand of their needs and expectations. We can even go as far as stating clearly how our activity will match their principal goals. This way, we'll be seen as indispensable to that success. The clearer the link, the better the job gets done. In the long run, we become more resilient and our longevity will be safer when things get tough. Resilience and longevity are both a matter of value in other people's eyes, so we need to measure up.

We're often being told to be a 'company man' (or person). Does this mean that we need to sell our souls for the privilege of the contract? Absolutely not.

This is an agreement, and both parties are seeking to get some value from it. But it doesn't mean giving up our goals and value to the exclusive gain of the other party.

Be mutual

In Victorian Britain, employees were paid in company tokens, not cash. They could only spend those tokens at the company stores within the company villages. Food, clothing, household goods all had to come from the company store. The employers effectively controlled every aspect of their employees' lives and they, in turn, were locked into the company's fortunes.

That style died out with the emergence of Trade Unions and employment legislation at the beginning of the 20th century. It was thought to be a feature of the 'dark old days' and long gone.

Interestingly, I'm seeing it re-emerge, in the modern companies of the high-tech industries of Silicon Valley. Companies like Google, Microsoft, Facebook and LinkedIn are now providing a 'total wrap-around' for their employees. They provide out-of-town campuses and lay on high-quality dining and recreational facilities on site. Employees are seduced into remaining on campus for most, if not all, of their day and they eat, socialise and shop effectively in 'the company store' once more.

Yes, these companies pay high salaries to the brightest and best. Many of these employees go out and buy expensive cars to take themselves to and from designer apartment blocks in the gentrifying downtown suburbs of San Francisco, Seattle or Portland. These developments effectively become high-tech, expensive, ghettos for the IT elite. Company culture prevails.

Many have gone one step further and created on-site accommodation, within the campuses, for their young, bright-eyed, highly-qualified professionals. They go straight from the college dorm into the company village.

Are we returning to the patriarchal control of the Victorian era - except, maybe, this time, with T-shirts and loafers?

We don't all work for huge global enterprises, yet the demand to take over more and more of our lives is increasing.

It may be overt or subtle, but the pressure to conform is definitely growing. It remains our own responsibility to strike the right work-life balance for ourselves, in the face of ever-growing demands upon us.

It's down to us to remember our own value expectations in return.

Be diligent

At some point we will settle on an agreement and work can begin. Once we decide to engage with a value exchange, the dynamic changes. We might have chosen to invest large parts of our time and energies in work.

We have struck a deal that is based around an exchange of value: creativity and labour for cash and benefits. At that point, our long-term goals become moot or unimportant.

Right then, we need to suspend our own desire for reward and apply ourselves to our immediate commitments. We know that we have a life beyond work, and we need to maintain those boundaries, as we dedicate ourselves to the task in hand. At that point, delivering value becomes our goal, and we need to do that, as well as we've agreed to.

As a life coach, I take care to explain what will happen in sessions with my clients. We agree on the fees and the times, and take care of business before the session.

Once the session begins, my whole focus is given to my client. The world, my business and the rest of my life disappears, and the client receives my full attention.

"A dream doesn't become reality through magic; it takes sweat, determination and hard work."

Colin Powell
U.S. Secretary of State, Joint Chiefs of Staff, four-star general

Once the session ends, I pick up my life again and get on with it and my business. During the agreed client time, the client is all that exists.

Even future aspirations need to be put to one side. Our future career, and resilience, will take care of itself over the longer term. While working on an agreed job, that's all that matters. Of course, good performance in the immediate task will go a long way to securing future advances, but thinking of those only acts as a distraction to doing a good job right now. In short, we need to commit to now, the short term, before we can reach the long term.

Of course, we can't lose sight of our bigger goals, but they will only be achieved one step at a time. The only step that we can take is the one in front of us right now. So we need to step up to the agreed needs of the other party, and subsume our own, for now.

Our dreams will happen as a by-product of giving ourselves fully to the task in hand, for others to achieve their dream goals. This kind of shift in commitment will show up in our communications, our interaction, and our approach to work. Do this for one day, our management will take notice; do it for two weeks and we will become an invaluable asset. Career resilience happens in every moment, not at year's end during our annual review.

Be timely

You might be wondering about what I mean by 'short term'. How long is the short term? Well it's now, and every moment is precious.

I've found that many people forget to clarify duration in any agreement. Working hours, for example, might be 35 or 40 hours per week. Yet how many people do we see working 60 or 70 hours a week? Salaried staff, in particular, get caught in this trap.

Once again, it's down to us, individually, to set our boundaries. When it's time to go home, go home. The work will still be there tomorrow. If it's a deadline, we can negotiate some time off 'in lieu' once the rush has passed. And I know that's tough. Employers and other taskmasters are very skilled at squeezing more from us. It could be in the form of a guilt trip or even veiled threats.

Typically, it's because they are fearful of their own pressures. We don't need to fall into that fear with them. After all, we're usually being paid for our labour, not as a rescuer. If they need rescuing, that needs to be their problem, not ours.

All too easily, we can fall into what I call 'chronic rescuer syndrome', where everybody else's problems become ours. So, quite simply, let's not be a rescuer. Do what we agreed and keep the scope and duration within bounds.

"Talent wins games, but teamwork and intelligence wins championships."

Michael Jordan

Professional basketball player, businessman

Be effective

Time is money and it's the scarcest commodity we have. If we want to maximise our value to others we need to make sure that we are spending our time wisely. That means two things: first, focus on what's important (to them) and, second, work effectively.

Notice I'm saying effectively, not efficiently. Resilience and adding value are about delivering outcomes: effectiveness focuses on the outcome while efficiency focuses on the process. If the process is heading in the wrong direction or is convoluted and awkward, doing it faster is of less value than making it better.

All too often, we are charged with delivering output, rather than outcomes, and there's a big difference.

If you remember, we made a distinction between leaders and managers. Leaders are interested in vision and outcomes; managers are interested in process and output.

So when we discuss value, it'll be wise to make the differentiation between goals and targets.

Goals that deliver outcomes are big-picture, visionary goals. They are delivered through working effectively.

Targets drive output results - they operate at a much lower level of processes and tasks.

Let's be clear about the level at which we're working. Are we machine monkeys, driving a process and churning out pieces? Or are we leaders, delivering value towards visionary goals?

Of course, we may be either, or both, at any point in time. It's important to understand which we are doing and deliver appropriately. At work, we may be processing production items, but it's for our number one client.

Priority, quality and timescale may take on a special importance in this case.

We're giving it top priority for the greater goal of retaining a valued customer. That is, 'valued' because they bring in our best source of livelihood.

Again, let's be clear, special means special... and exceptional. Our extra effort is extra. This, by definition, does not mean ordinary or every day. When does normal service resume?

At home, we may simply be pushing the vacuum cleaner around, or we may be tidying up the house to welcome visitors. Which is the target and which is the goal? I know I do a better job of vacuuming when I know that I have guests coming.

When we focus on results, we become committed to the task at hand. When we focus on outcomes, we'll make sure that each task is performed at optimum quality.

Eventually, we become embedded in a bigger value system and become indispensable. Our resilience and longevity will increase even further. We become much less likely to be debating about whether to quit or not.

Be constant

Value is not a one-hit wonder and we should be striving constantly to add value. In fact, if we want to assure longevity and ongoing commitment, we might want to increase the pace. That will require our understanding, and acceptance, of continuous change. There's an old adage, *'You're only as good as your last performance'* and it's never been truer than in the modern world.

Yesterday's income has been counted and taken to the bank already. The news cycle has dropped from weekly to daily and now to instantaneously. Yesterday's results are already old news. Look forward to how we are going to add even more value.

Of course, when doing more is required, doing more of the same is the easiest way... keep delivering the expected value.

But those are basic table stakes and the bidding is going up, not down. Expectations are constantly growing, towards increasing value; delivering more today than we did yesterday. It may mean no more than improving efficiency and turning out more cycles from the same process.

"It is the service we are not obliged to give that people value most."

James Cash Penney
(American businessman and entrepreneur)

If it isn't broken, don't fix it. If the process is working well, there's little scope or need to change it at all. There's little value, and maybe even a little danger, in tinkering with a well-oiled machine.

Be selective

An even more important part of our value will be in how we can deliver more than 'business as usual'. So we should always be looking for ways to add extra value, not merely contributing to today's success. That's where understanding the overall goals, not merely the required task results, comes into play.

We need to be circumspect in what we seek to 'improve'. Peripheral processes that cost money and effort, but deliver very little value, are easy targets. Nobody important will worry about eliminating those marginal tasks, and any cost, time or effort reductions will be welcomed.

There's always scope to eliminate unnecessary activities, which add little or no value. Just stop doing them. Core processes, on the other hand, are fraught with danger. They are highly visible, they make major contributions to the bottom line, and they are probably 'owned' by someone very important. So, in these instances, we need to tread carefully, when seeking to change them.

The boss will probably have been doing the same thing, the same way, for years and he'll see little need to change it. Mostly, he'll be resisting any change to anything that affects him, or is likely to affect him, personally.

Closer to home, imagine trying to suggest to your partner that there's a better way to hang out the laundry - never an easy conversation. But what if the change you are suggesting could shave, say, half-an-hour per load in hanging, folding and even ironing? Now they'll be listening.

Strategic change is risky but, when chosen wisely, can pay dividends to the bottom line, and to everybody's value. Our own resilience and growth will be aligned to that of others in the agreement, at work or anywhere else. Embracing change, when done strategically and well, can turn out to be a real win-win for everybody involved.

I suggest that we set out by winning support and buy-in, before attempting change to an embedded activity. When, and if, we pull it off, the changes can deliver significant added value and our prestige should climb accordingly.

Be a keeper

Security is largely about the here and now. Resilience and longevity, however, is all about the future. We'll only be the kind of people that our partners, friends and employers want to have around, in the future, if they can see value from us over the longer term.

If we are viewed like that, we'll be seen as assets and be invested in: if not, we'll be treated as resources and consumed in the here and now.

Our efforts will be taken in the moment and our empty husks will be discarded when we're done. Once spent, resources are replaced as commodities. None of us wants to be consumed and thrown away as having no further value.

Our longevity is based on what we can deliver in the future, not simply what we do today. What's more, the people that we're trying to develop for, in the long term, need to understand our long-term worth.

There's a subtle change in orientation when we move ourselves from being a human resource to being human capital.

We should always be reassuring those around us about our value in contribution to that future vision. Our longevity depends upon being viewed as an asset, not a commodity. That's the difference in being a 'human capital' rather than a 'human resource'.

One gets consumed, the other is invested in and treasured.

We can make that shift from resource to capital with clear communication, direct positioning and clear speaking within a vision.

Our understanding of future plans will allow us to demonstrate, today, that we should be part of the future. Showing that we understand the importance of what we're doing, and suggesting how it can be maintained and extended, will lock us into the hearts and minds of those with whom we're exchanging value.

It's easy to be inquisitive and excited by the bigger picture, so ask about it.

Whether it's about new ideas at work, or the ways a dinner party can be made better, our enthusiasm will be infectious. We'll find ourselves included in the forward thinking of future plans.

What's more, we'll secure our place in the future, and even build a better slot for ourselves in that future.

How cool would that be?

What would that do for our longer-term resilience?

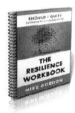

Remember to download your free

Resilience

Workbook

Just follow the link below.

http://mikegordonbooks.com/download-sig-workbook/

You'll need the password that you find, at the end of Chapter 12

CHAPTER 6: NETWORK VALUE

"Sometimes, idealistic people are put off the whole business of networking as something tainted by flattery and the pursuit of selfish advantage. But virtue in obscurity is rewarded only in Heaven. To succeed in this world, you have to be known to people."

Sonia Sotomayor
US Supreme Court Justice

We've been looking at the whole idea of building resilience, success and staying power, through recognising and building what is of value to ourselves.

We've also looked at the giving and receiving of value with others.

It's probably time to think about the opportunities to create and share that value. That's where the whole idea of networking value comes into play.

So before we dive into network value, let's understand what we mean by networks and how they work.

The dictionaries give us these definitions:

NETWORK

> *A group or system of interconnected people or things. A group of people who exchange information and contacts for professional or social purposes.*

Oxford Dictionaries

> *A group of people or organizations that are closely connected and that work with each other.*

Merriam-Webster Dictionary

> *An association of individuals having a common interest, formed to provide mutual assistance, helpful information, or the like.*

Dictionary.com

They all share the common factor of being made up of multiple people, or things, and extend this to include some purpose of sharing and exchange. For our purposes, I would like to take this one stage further, to suggest that the exchanges within the network are purposeful... to give and get value in terms each networked individual will recognise.

This last element adds a fundamental distinction to the reason, and manner, in which we connect to others in our value network. Our value networks have a purpose. There will be qualification criteria for membership, and value exchange needs to occur.

With our value networks, we're not talking about the myriad, often random, contacts we make throughout our everyday lives. No, we're talking about connections that we have chosen to make, with a clear purpose, and with people who meet our qualification criteria.

Think of a drinks party or an evening in the pub. We'll meet our regular friends and be delighted to be with them. We'll also meet new people of whom we have little or no previous experience. And that's where so-called 'small talk' kicks in.

"No man is an island, entire of itself; every man is a piece of the continent, a part of the main"

John Donne
English poet (1572-1631)

Most often, we'll be introduced to them by someone already in our network. We'll greet them, shake hands, 'air kiss' them or whatever, with a smile on our faces.

We engage in a little informal chatting and general exploration of who they are and what their interests might be. We want to get to know them – a little.

Whether it's a deliberate tactic, or simply social instincts, we are scoping these new people out. We're scanning them to gauge if they're going to have value for us. We're making an early evaluation of their worth to us. We're not necessarily judging if they are worthy overall, but whether they present the kind of opportunities that we value.

For some of us, this social mixing is easy; for others it's a real strain. What's more, there may even be a gender angle to it. Madeleine Albright was US Secretary of State and a 'professional socialiser' in diplomatic circles. She reckons that men and women go about connecting in different ways:

"I think women are really good at making friends and not good at networking. Men are good at networking and not necessarily making friends. That's a gross generalisation, but I think it holds in many ways."

Madeleine Albright
Former US Secretary of State

Whichever way we feel about it, I would argue that, if our networks are going to bring us value, we will want to become good at networking: meeting people, evaluating their 'worth' to us, connecting, engaging and exchanging value with them.

As a small boy, I used to resist going grocery shopping with my grandmother. It was torture.

Every 10 steps she'd bump into someone she knew and would stop for a 'quick chat'. I'd be left swinging on her hand, getting more and more bored, frustrated and truculent.

Then it was into the butcher's shop, the baker's, the greengrocer's and the fishmonger's. She simply had to catch up with the latest news from every single person. She'd also be exchanging what she'd just learned in the earlier encounters. The whole trip seemed interminable.

If she had given me a shopping list and the money, I could probably have completed the entire shopping in 15 minutes. But that simply wasn't the point. To my grandmother, doing the shopping was much more.

For her, it was like reading the newspaper, watching the evening news on TV and catching up on Facebook, all rolled into one. She was the ultimate social networker long before the internet or mobile phones were invented... and she was an expert!

If ever my grandmother needed something to be done, she'd know exactly the right person to do it. It would be someone's nephew or daughter, or next door neighbour. She'd be able to engage them for the task and even exert social pressure to get it done as quickly and cheaply as possible. She had established her personal value to her network and was able to call on it for support when needed. Her networks were both purposeful and valuable.

This introduces another fundamental attribute of networks. The connections are diffuse; they are not simply point to point. We talk about a circle of friends, a group of colleagues or a guild of tradespeople. There is an added value in belonging to a group that is more than simply a set of one-to-one transactions.

How often do we hear business owners talk about their firm being like a family? They know that, when people feel connected in a network structure, they will feel more engaged, and ultimately be more creative.

In those environments, work becomes more than a linear process with clear-cut hand-offs or single individual transactions.

Those bosses actively encourage diffuse connections, across multiple activities, in a spirit of sharing and collaboration. Work is changing to become more like the real world environment, not so much the corporate jungle, as a professional ecosystem.

What's more, each of us will have multiple networks in our lives. They will serve different purposes and provide us with different kinds of value: family support, work advancement, social release and many more. The purpose may be different, but many of the general characteristics will be the same.

Networks can exist at work, at home, socialising, in club memberships, or whatever else. If network colleagues see value in knowing us, they will support us and build our own value and resilience without even knowing they're doing it. Just like my grandmother's situation, being invaluable in the lives of the other network members will pay dividends to us, now and over the long term.

"Creating a better world requires teamwork, partnerships, and collaboration. We need an entire army of companies and people to work together to build a better world. This means (we) must embrace the benefits of cooperating with one another."

Simon Mainwaring
Branding consultant, social media specialist, blogger

Indeed, the networks themselves can be regarded as having a life of their own. They are organic, they have unique mechanisms, are self-nurturing and maintain a balanced internal ecosystem. Belonging to a network is much more than having a set of individual friends or associates.

Our value to the world expands as our networks develop and grow.

So let's get networking. It's really quite simple and there are a few relatively straightforward steps, which we can take to build and work our networks. The rest of this chapter will explore the main ones.

Get connected

In a people-driven world, we need to be able to fit in with those around us and help to build value; for them, the organisation and ourselves. Over the long term, those with strong interpersonal relationships will be far more likely to get chosen to be part of groups that get things done.

The best of them will be most likely to be chosen for leadership roles. Strong networking is one of the most effective winning strategies for personal resilience and security and overall longevity in what we want to do.

"The richest people in the world look for and build networks; everyone else looks for work."

Robert Kiyosaki
Businessman, investor, author, educator

Let's face it, companies don't hire people... people hire people. The workplace and job market are all about relationships. People, not companies, come up with ideas.

People, not organisations, make processes work. Even the most automated production lines need people to make them work well. Relationships make the workplace flow smoothly, so let's engage the power of many.

Interesting and interested

In everyday life, our main sources of value live inside our networks. Value networking starts with mutually beneficial relationships with the people nearest to us; in our families, clubs, work departments and teams.

Earn their respect and trust and they'll become the sales team of our personal brand. They'll promote our value to the network and the network will reward us with opportunity, support and its own added value.

Standing alone will simply exclude us from all of that value.

When we're curious about their world, and show an interest in the opportunities that they see on the horizon, they will expose new opportunities for us. It may be deliberate or unintentional, but we'll get early sight of what's moving.

Broader relationships, across the wider reach of those organisations, will extend our reputation further.

That will put us in line for new opportunities, by getting to know those with the power to enhance our progress. The same goes for those who can spot opportunities, which we might not see, from our immediate position.

In my own case, I was heavily involved with the Global Diversity Council at my last corporate firm.

It had very little to do with my everyday job but it was part of my 'give back' and leadership for the company as a whole.

In truth, my activity and connection in the Diversity Council worried many of my direct bosses. They could see me communicating all over the world with Country General Managers and Executive Vice-Presidents. They were partly nervous and generally jealous of the access this work gave me.

Ultimately, it was this level of connection that secured my move from Europe to Australia. I was here on vacation, and stopped by for an informal coffee and a 'hands across the seas' chat with the local head of consulting for Asia.

Within 20 minutes of our meeting, he reached over with my resume and simply asked, "*So, Mike, when can you start?*"

I was flabbergasted.

Firstly, I had no intention of coming for a job interview.

Secondly, I could see that this was a foregone conclusion in his mind.

Finally, I realised that colleagues on the Council had set me up for my next big career shift without me being aware of it. The power of networks was bringing me value that I had no idea to expect.

When we get good at networking, we can begin to think of a network of networks. We have our immediate circles, with whom we interact on a daily basis. And each of those daily associates will have broader networks of their own. Once we're trusted in our direct network it'll become natural to be introduced more widely to new networks, which we might never have considered on our own.

So, my work on the Global Diversity Council led to an introduction, and a recommendation, to the head of Consulting for Asia-Pacific. That led to a new career opportunity which I probably would not have achieved directly. My direct network had much a wider reach than I could possibly have alone.

Network of networks

A network of networks is very much like that drinks party. We know our own people and, because they like and trust us, they will introduce us to their wider circles. And, just like those new introductions, we can engage in a little small talk and do some sounding out.

This time, it'll be with the organism that is the new network, beyond simply the individual person within it. We'll be scoping out the purpose, goals and values of that new network, as manifest by the people in it. It's much more than simply deciding if we like an individual, but rather, it's deciding if we like what they represent, and whether it offers each of us value.

That's how it was with my Australian opportunity. It was a huge potential change for me and I took the time to explore the wider implications. In the end, I decided that the upside was far more valuable than any mere dislocation and inconvenience.

Our resilience is strengthened by the breadth and depth of the relationships, from across all of our interests. Let others enhance our personal brand, strengthen our reputation, and propel us forward.

"You can design and create, and build the most wonderful place in the world. But it takes people to make the dream a reality."

Walt Disney
Founder, Walt Disney Studios, film director

Then there are external networks to develop. There are plenty of networks out there that could bring us our heart's desires and life's goals. It's just that we're not connected into them... yet.

It's exactly those external networks that can help us to sustain our ambitions for bigger change, and support growth to new horizons. Simply put, we need less of our own resilience, if others are prepared to give us a helping hand, or boost us to the next level.

It starts now

All the talk in the world is just that... talk. Actions speak louder than words. If we want to see progress and start to get value, we should be getting more directly, and personally, involved. We should be going to events, seeking introductions and joining relevant groups that fit our goals.

It's time to get out there and spread the love. In our careers, for example, professional associations, membership clubs and networking sites (like LinkedIn) are great ways to promote our personal brands and identify new opportunities.

By now our localised networking has taught us about our broader aims and activities. We are clear about what we need, and want, to develop and make our dreams a reality. So identifying who we need to develop in our networks becomes more obvious.

If it's about exchanging knowledge and insight in the network - we can recruit personal mentors or offer mentoring to others. We can support friends, colleagues and even casual acquaintances in their projects. In return, they will be more inclined to offer their support, and to inspire us during our hard times, or in our own plans. They might just be the bridge to the next major opportunity.

Demonstrating our value to others, through practical experiences, is a great way to have them open doors for us.

Remember, investing a little of our resilience and effort, to kick-start an exchange of value, will pay us back in the longer term.

There's no time like the present; get connected now. We know that strong connections and collaboration are good for us and for getting the big stuff done. We connect with the best of intentions. It's honourable. So why do we hold back?

Like Sonia Sotomayor implies, in the quote at the beginning of this chapter, do we feel that networking is somehow grubby or self-serving? Do we feel like we're being manipulative and exploitative? Well, sure we can choose to be exploitative of others but we've already realised that tactics like that are very short-lived.

There's no need to feel dishonourable when we are actively seeking to share our value. We're not looking for a free ride, or simply to coat-tail on other people's success. Instead, we should be keen to get out there and offer our value to others.

While we're at it, let's be clear that everyone in those networks will be doing exactly the same. They're out there looking for value for themselves. We'll soon learn if they share our desire for a mutual exchange of value. If they're looking for a free ride, it's easy enough to spot it and simply walk away. We're not mugs and we don't need to play a mug's game.

"The time to build a network is always before you need one."

Douglas Conant
President, CEO, Campbell Soup Company

Now is the time to act. If we wait until there's a crisis or we've become desperate, our chances of success will be so much less.

Leaving contacts until they're needed makes others doubt our motives and cynicism creeps in when we do reach out. How often have you heard the comment:

'I never see him/her until s/he needs something?'

And what kind of tone is it said in?

No, never pleasant.

Developing strong networks, of positive relationships, before we need them, reduces the cynicism and engenders a positive predisposition to collaborate - we can start to extend our circles of contacts now, in a planned and methodical way, without waiting until there's a crisis.

Building the resilience fund starts today.

Expressing gratitude

When we've begun to engage in our networks, that's also the time to share the joy - it's the perfect opportunity to truly appreciate others and recognise their contributions to us. When we show real gratitude to our network colleagues, we deepen the bonds with them.

So it's never weakness to show some gratitude to those around us.

Far from putting us at a disadvantage, our own reputations will increase, our networks will extend and we'll grow even further.

There are many ways to express gratitude and I see three quite specific opportunities to do so.

1. Value the presence of others:

Interdependence is unavoidable, and we will do well to appreciate contributions that directly, or indirectly, impact our work for good. Appreciation makes others feel glad that they helped you; it makes them more willing to help again and even more likely to keep supporting you positively.

Neglecting the kind of value that different people bring to us risks alienation, resentment and resistance. And negative opinions will only harm our long-term viability. Just try to get support from those guys when you've been ignoring them all year!

No chance.

In my book writing example, my author connections did very little direct work for me or the book. Typically, our interaction was over a cup of coffee, and fairly general. But their support and encouragement got me started and kept me going. It had a tangible impact on me, and the book, I was grateful for it and expressed it freely.

2. Value an individual's work:

Accepting, and appreciating, such work doesn't make us any less capable, or less valuable, ourselves. In fact, with the help of colleagues, we'll be able to focus on our own work more effectively, because there's someone else doing their job well.

Once again, with this book, those supporting me were working professionally for a fee. It wasn't charity, or simple friendship.

Nonetheless, I was keen to keep the work collaborative and appreciative. When problems or glitches cropped up, we were able to work things out quickly and amicably, and get back on track.

Nobody can write a contract for that interpersonal collaboration and cooperation, but just try getting a book produced without it.

I am very grateful for the manner in which we worked together as much as for the fact that I have been able to write the material which we worked upon.

Being grateful of what others are doing with, and for, us, encourages them to do more of it and offers us even more opportunities.

Even when they see it as simply doing their job, our recognition keeps the process moving along more smoothly.

We tip waiters for good service (when it's arguably part of their job) and think nothing of it. Why wouldn't we tip our closest friends and colleagues with a simple 'thanks'?

That's like my reader's panel. They were helping me out as friends and acquaintances. They got early sight of my book, before it was published, and I got feedback and ideas from my 'typical' audience.

It was a win-win without money exchange.

The fuel that kept this going was dialogue and gratitude.

3. Value teamwork:

Teamwork is the key to the success of any project or organisation. Irrespective of the significance of our own contribution, it does not, and cannot, stand alone.

We need to be interconnected, in modern life and workplaces, and teams are at the core of our own personal success. So embrace teamwork; open up to sharing ideas, work in collaboration.

Once again, writing this book offers a great example. I had a number of professionals working on different aspects of the book at different times. They were usually as one-to-one dialogues with me. Towards the end of the production phase we needed to form one holistic view of the whole entity.

I'm delighted that each of the professionals were able to come together to finalise the details and how they impacted on each other's work.

I facilitated the team but had little input to offer personally. If this book looks like a well-crafted item, it's entirely thanks to their collaboration and teamwork.

Understanding, and using, our team's dynamics will get a more creative, effective and valuable outcome, usually quicker and at less cost. And the more teams we can be part of, the more our reputation will grow.

Isn't it better to be known widely as 'the person that works well with others and gets things done', than the opposite; the stand-off loner who grabs all of the attention for themselves?

Teamwork builds our reputation and makes us more likely to be the one who stays and thrives during tough times.

Remember, building teamwork has its own dynamic of 'forming, norming, storming and performing'. It's necessary and it works.

Networking means people

So far, we've been thinking about networks as being people connecting with people... and so it should be. Today, however, if we talk about networking, many people's minds immediately jump to electronic media.

Don't get me wrong, I love electronic media and I pretty much couldn't live without it these days. Electronic media is a boon to modern society in so many ways, but it has one serious drawback... it is reducing and limiting the prevalence of one-to-one, face-to-face interaction and the richness this offers to our lives.

Communicating with people is an opportunity to build relationships with them, not only to transfer information.

With all of the forms of electronic communication available today, our conversations are becoming more and more clipped, impersonal - and actually less effective. Texts, emails, voicemails and conferencing are allowing us to introduce gulfs in both time and geography. They even allow us to avoid contact with each other altogether.

My advice and practice, wherever possible, is to get real: to choose real communication over e-communication. Make time to meet people in person, to look them in the eye and relate to them. I strongly believe it pays dividends.

The richness of the content with face-to-face is much, much greater than with any other medium. In addition, the simple act of investing time and effort to be with someone is hugely rewarding. It sends out a great signal of their worth to you. So, if we want to build real networks and valued relationships, we need to get real with people.

I know it's not always possible to meet in person. I have many clients in remote locations that I work with via electronic media. As a minimum, I seek to use desktop video conferencing such as Skype or FaceTime, from a full screen computer. At least that way we can pick up each other's facial cues and body language.

We all know that most (around 80 per cent) of our interaction is based on non-verbal communications and signals.

Video helps us to retain much of that non-verbal interaction as we communicate. Retention diminishes rapidly as we slide down the 'richness' scale of other electronic media. Voice calls come a poor second after video. Next would be instant messaging, email, voicemail and finally, at the bottom of the heap, SMS texting.

And yet, what do we see all over the world? People hitting their phones to text remote friends - their 'chat' is so important that it even over-rides communicating with people sitting right there with them. I sigh when I see whole lunch tables of colleagues glued to their phones and snatching bites of food in between texts.

I get tired of people walking straight into me in the street because they're not looking where they're going. I sometimes just stand my ground and let it happen. The looks on their faces are priceless.

Somehow, they want to blame me for not moving out of their way. Their bodies are in one place but their lives are somewhere else. And somehow, that's my fault? I'm supposed to look after their physical presence, in a way that they are not prepared to do for themselves?

No, I don't remember signing up to that particular social contract.

Texting even takes over in life-threatening situations. I simply can't understand why someone judges that replying to a text message is more important to their lives than keeping their eyes on the road when driving, or crossing the street. Texting while driving or walking is now costing lives... lives of the texter and those of their crash victims.

Networking is valuable... but not if you're dead.

I'm sure that the text junkies think of themselves as excellent networkers. My view is that they are fundamentally confusing quantity for quality. Non-stop chatter is very different from quality conversation and the same is true for real and virtual networking.

Nurture the network

Finally, we've been linking our networking activity to our value system.

So let's be protective - just as networking can build value when done wisely, so too can it destroy value.

We're busy building positive value, and the last thing we need is the drag of negativity and untrustworthiness. Trust your intuition: eliminate the naysayers.

The biggest giants in the business world will tell you that they rely heavily on their 'gut'.

So should we. It's natural, powerful and part of our evolutionary makeup.

"The toughest thing about the power of trust is that it's very difficult to build and very easy to destroy. The essence of trust-building is to emphasise the similarities between you."

Thomas J. Watson
Chairman, CEO: International Business Machines (IBM)

Our intuition about people can be a true asset in our business and personal lives.

If it feels like someone is up to no good, they probably are.

Our feelings about people are based on subtle but powerful cues. All too often, we dismiss and undervalue our intuition, because we can't be precise about justifying it.

Our intuition is really messages arising in our unconscious minds and arriving in our conscious minds.

We're not sure how they got there, and that uncertainty can lead us to dismiss those messages as meaningless.

Nurture your intuition

Learning to hear and develop our intuition can be helpful in lots of different moments, across the day.

Here are three of the best ones:

1. Build clusters of positivity

Some personalities will work well together, but not all. Some people cannot, or will not, get on board. And we don't need to spend an inordinate amount of time trying to convince them to join in.

We can give them an opportunity to correct their negative attitudes but, if they persist, we can remove them from the group or project. There are not enough hours in the day to convert someone who has convinced themselves that they don't want to follow the plan.

Remember, shared success depends upon strong teamwork.

2. Avoid the critics

That is, those who are constantly trying to catch your mistakes, those who only see a downside to your work, and never offer constructive ideas for improvement.

They'll be the ones sucking air through their teeth, folding their arms and slowly shaking their head. We can be more assertive in stopping their negativity or we can simply walk away. We can turn it around by asking them what would make it better.

How can they help to make it better? Usually, they'll have no useful answers, because that was never their purpose in criticising.

Typically, they're trying to elevate themselves by pulling us lower. If left unchecked, they will undermine our resilience and reputation.

Simply walk away.

3. Avoid the time-wasters

Spot the colleagues who love to gossip and spread rumours. We'll see them at the water cooler or around the photocopier at work, in the kitchen at home, or hanging around on street corners.

Such people tend to emphasise the negative things over the positive. One negative person or event can tear down months of motivation or reputation in minutes. Again, they have little to contribute, and would rather undervalue other people's contributions than make one for themselves. They have little sense of what value is and little intention of creating or sharing any.

We can simply walk away and lose nothing of value.

Networks produce value

We've been looking at value, and how giving, and getting, value can build our resilience, and maintain our momentum in whatever we're doing.

We've also seen that value exchange is best done in networks of people, beyond simple one-to-one transactions. And finally, we've explored the ways in which we can develop and sustain our place in those valued networks.

By now you'll have guessed that I'm a big fan of developing and maintaining strong networks. And I'm truly grateful to have them and the people in them. They add real value to me and make life easier in so many ways. In writing this book,

I've found professional support such as editors, designers, layout specialists, photographers, - all via personal recommendations from my networks. I've had a reader's panel, to read the material in advance of publishing, drawn from my many social networks. I've even had encouragement and support from other authors, which got me started in the first place.

In a real sense, you wouldn't be reading this book today if it weren't for my networks and the people in them.

I hope this has given you the confidence to value the people around you more, and to see the incremental value of having them as your network.

Sharing your connections will only add to your strength and resilience. It will increase the opportunities to grow and will drive success and value towards you. Jealously guarding relationships or knowledge will ultimately diminish us and our worth.

So go on, be bold. Have fun. Start networking.

 **Remember to download your free**

Resilience

Workbook

Just follow the link below.

http://mikegordonbooks.com/download-siq-workbook/

You'll need the password that you find, at the end of Chapter 12

CHAPTER 7: LEFT, RIGHT AND CENTRE

> "Intuition is the wisdom formed by feeling and instinct - a gift of knowing without reasoning... Belief is ignited by hope and supported by facts and evidence - it builds alignment and creates confidence. Belief is what sets energy in motion and creates the success that breeds more success."
>
> **Angela Ahrendts**
> **Businesswoman Executive Apple Inc. and Burberry**

We're about half-way through the exploration of whether we should quit or not, and we've covered a lot of ground already. So far, we've looked at questions of direction, value and resilience. We've considered strategies for staying where we are and making it work better for us.

I firmly recommend that our first approach to difficult times and situations is to stay put, to review what's really going on and to consider our options, before simply quitting. There may come a point, however, where moving on might turn out to be the best answer.

It becomes a decision about change, rather than one about quitting. Moving on to new things is always more exciting than simply giving up on what we're doing today.

We shouldn't shrink away from change, but we should be making clear and positive decisions, about how to change, and to what. It becomes a question more about what we're moving to, than what we're running from. So, if we're now all about change, this will be a good time to be clear about looking at change and making positive choices.

Positive change can be uplifting, inspiring and good. Running away from a situation feels negative, like having failed in some way, or not being up to the challenges at hand.

So let's banish ideas of quitting, and embrace the notion of positive change.

Let's start with a quick question about our current situation. A top of the mind answer is our best indication here. Be quick, don't think about it,

"How do I feel about what I'm doing these days?"

What's the first answer that comes to mind? Do we feel energised by it, drained by it or nothing at all?

If it's 'energised', then we're probably doing OK and not thinking about quitting. If it's either of the other two, it may be time to consider moving on and doing something different.

The question was specifically asking about how we feel about our situation. That's because our perceptions end up as feelings and inevitably guide our decision making. Every decision that we ever make is an emotional one.

We may believe, especially in business, that we can make purely rational decisions. Sorry, lovely reader, it's simply not true. All decisions are based on emotions, and our emptions are driven by our perception of the world around us. So, if we're thinking of quitting, it's because we feel bad and those feelings are driven by our reading of the outside world.

We may have some concrete facts, that make us unhappy about where we are, but the facts quickly turn into feelings.

We may have an uneasy instinct about the situation and we end up feeling uncomfortable. Our instincts are driven by comparing the current situation with our lives up to now. Those unconscious comparisons surface as yet more feelings. Or we may simply tap directly into our feelings and know that we're unhappy, without even questioning why or how. All of these feelings are based on our perceptions of the world around us.

By understanding where our perceptions come from, we'll be able to understand what's driving our feelings, and that will help us make clearer and better decisions.

This chapter will explore how our minds work and the way that we perceive the world. That understanding will help us to tap into our perceptions and ultimately help us decide whether to stay or go. We'll be able to know what's driving our feelings, and cut through to a deeper understanding of what's really going on.

Hardware or software

Firstly, let's distinguish between our brains and our minds. Our brain is a physical organ in the body. It's made up of cells of various kinds; it needs a blood supply, has physical and chemical processes, breathes oxygen and burns energy, just like any other organ in our bodies. Our brains respond to physical stimuli and generate signals to our bodies and minds.

Our minds are altogether more mysterious. It's more of a conceptual idea, rather than a physical entity. It processes our thoughts, memories and feelings. So, weirdly, the mind is a product of its own self. It's where our perceptions lie.

Whenever we have a thought, feeling or action, it's the result of our brains receiving input signals, making a connection and putting out another signal to our minds and bodies.

It's as if our brains are the hardware of our perceptions and our minds are the software that runs on it. They work together to produce our thoughts and feelings, as outputs. This is the stuff of perceptions.

Traditionally, our perceptions have been related to the shape of our brains; a left hemisphere, a right hemisphere and our lower or core brain.

It's a simple way of relating our active minds to what's going on in our physical brains and can help us to spotlight our thoughts and feelings more clearly.

Some older thinking suggested that we were limited to being primarily left-brained, right-brained or intuitive (limbic). More up-to-date research suggests that we're all omni-brained and that we actually engage all of our brains, all of the time.

Neuro-physiologists routinely scan brains, and can see activity sparking across all areas of our brains when we are thinking, or doing anything.

So let's bust the myth about us only using 10% of our brains and that we can unlock superpowers by engaging more of our brain's activity. It's already engaged.

Neuro-scientists now have the concept of 'centres of activity' in our brains. Each centre is responsible for registering physical senses, controlling activity and even thinking, remembering and generating emotions. The centres have complex interactions in response to stimuli, where multiple centres are active at any one time.

That's a view based purely at the 'hardware' level, and our perceptions also involve the 'software' level of our minds. It's our minds that tap into the multiple brain centres and create a mental picture of our situation. That's our perception.

There is decades of research into how we perceive the world and there's a broad consensus, in psycho-cognitive circles, of how we interpret the world.

It suggests that we perceive the world in three fundamentally different ways, which we'll call left, right and centre. And here, we're talking about our minds, not simply the physical brain. So really, we're now talking about being left, right or centre minded, not brained.

Three minds

For the rest of this chapter, we'll look at how our minds perceive the world, rather than our brains. We'll focus on left, right and centre minded activity, rather than on what the physical brain is doing.

Our left mind is our analytical zone. It takes in information from the world, and applies logic, structure and process to what we perceive. It's analytical and interested in facts, numbers, plans, processes, structures and sequences. It processes detail.

Our right mind deals more with overall shape and form. It sees the world more holistically, and is interested in shape, colours, emotions, patterns, interpersonal behaviours, and movement. It synthesises understanding.

Our core, or centre, mind is much more ancient and deals with deeper truths. It is our deepest memory bank and it's believed that we never actually forget anything that's happened in our lives, but we usually choose not to bring it to the fore.

Our centre mind is constantly matching patterns of what's happening now, to what we've encountered in the past. It draws inputs from both our left and right minds, and wraps them in the insights of our unconscious memories.

It measures situations with aspects like values, purpose, intuition and impulse. As such, it is our deepest safety check about what might be good or bad for us. It relates the world to what we believe, what we hold as fundamental to who we are. It's intuitive and builds on our core beliefs.

Each of us will have a preferred style of thinking and we usually bring that to the fore.

We all know people who are very analytical, and want to know facts, or people who are very creative or emotional, and want to understand how everything is moving along together. Then, there are those who seem very intuitive or spiritual, and tend to 'know' how the world is, without being bothered by mere detail.

Our best decisions emerge when we blend these three types of perception together.

Left-minded perceptions

The easiest place to start with understanding our perceptions is in our left mind. We live in an increasingly complex and regulated world. We are surrounded by rules and regulations, expectations from others and a whole host of metrics and measurements. It's not surprising that we become preoccupied with facts, processes and the way that 'things should be done'. This is squarely the left-minded aspect of life, and where we find ourselves living, for most of our day.

Since good judgements and decisions are based upon evidence, this will be a good place to look for evidence so that we can make some well-grounded decisions. Our left mind loves data, so let's give it some.

Data is very often represented by numbers, and has the benefit of being clear and simple. The answer is either, 5 or 6, 200 or 201 or 17.236 or 17.237. It doesn't really matter how detailed we make the number, what matters is the fact that we can measure it, accurately, and use it as evidence in our decision making.

So let's quantify the situation and get some real data for our minds to work on. And let's not worry too much about spurious levels of detail. Is 17.237 any more meaningful than a simple 17, or even a rounded up 20?

Often, a rounded up number will be enough for our decisions and too much detail can take us off in a tangent that isn't important to our decision making.

The data that we want to collect will depend upon the decisions we're trying to make. Often, a single measure will be enough for the simplest decisions. Let's not blind ourselves with too many numbers.

Basic numbers can include inputs - like hours of effort, travel time, or incidental costs like clothes, food or equipment. Then there are outputs - like financial reward, time saved or material goods delivered. These are all absolute numbers and stand alone in how we measure them.

Timing of the numbers can often be important. The fact that we can earn a million dollars over our lifetime matters much less than what we take home each week. Short-term measurement is a fundamental part of our everyday living. We need to be rewarded in the present, for the efforts that we're putting in today.

That reward will probably be measured against what we actually achieve today. So, we'd be smart to measure both our input and output, and balance them against each other, to check that value is flowing to us in the present – and that it's proportionate with what we had to put in to get it. Imbalances here are one of the most common sources of disgruntlement and most often a trigger to quit.

The numbers may be accurate, and absolute, but are they enough? Our reward may be fair and as we agreed, but it might simply be insufficient to meet our needs. There's a growing phenomenon of the 'working poor' where individuals are working two or three jobs and still can't feed the family well. A downward spiral to poverty is never acceptable and may be a signal to reconsider our options.

Of course, we might also be investing in longer-term gain. Investing in our future is a good thing, as long as it's a good investment and we can afford it today. We still need to be able to survive the short term, to get to the long term. Jam tomorrow isn't bread and butter today.

So, measuring how much we're investing (time, effort or money), should be balanced with the likelihood of it returning the rewards that we expect. We need to be absolutely certain that the investment we make today has a good chance of paying off, with acceptable returns, in an acceptable timeframe. Simply trusting that it will all come good in the future can let us down.

Now, not all left-minded considerations are based upon measurable numbers, but they are still worth building into the decision. These considerations can include physical wellbeing, fairness and growth.

We should never underestimate the importance of our wellbeing in what we're doing. There are two very direct left-mind indicators that we can look for.

Let's begin by checking in with our physical body. Are we exhausted at the end of our efforts? Is it constantly like that, or are there peaks and troughs? Are we able to live life when we're finished? Over-working to the point of destroying any other life is, ultimately, a waste of time and effort.

Over-exertion can also show up in our sleep, diets, hobbies, and social activity. Check out how often we end up slumped on the sofa at the end of the day, or in arguments with family, friends or colleagues. It's easy to see if our clothes are beginning to feel tight. We can track how often we actually do go to the gym, or how many league games we've missed. If we're constantly drained, our life will be too.

Physical abuse is never acceptable and is a clear sign to move on. If what we're doing is physically dangerous, and there's insufficient attention given to our safety, we should be stopping to consider. If we can make our life safer, then we should.

If it's simply never going to be safe, that's the point to evaluate our risks and consider moving away. And let's not forget emotional abuse, it's real, and wears us down just as much. Check for physical or psychological bullying, excessive demands or overload.

This brings us around to the basic fairness checks of parity, equity and boundaries.

If we're working at the same level and standard as everyone else, our rewards should be at least equal to our peers. My diversity work has pointed up significant inequities based on gender, race, and sexual orientation, age and many other factors.

There is growing support for equal treatment, and anti-discrimination, but, ultimately, it comes down to us, and our sense of fairness. We can benchmark against external situations of comparable demand through external associations and bodies.

We can take some comfort if we're in balance with others around us and take action if we're not.

If the demands on us keep growing, but the rewards don't, then we're in the wrong place. Value exchange should be two-sided and demand also lays responsibilities on the demander. If that's missing, it might be a signal to move on.

We usually agree a reasonable balance of input and reward, at the beginning of a situation, but changes creep up on us, all too easily. Build in checkpoints to review if the balance is still acceptable.

We have a good sense of what we deem to be practically and ethically acceptable. Often, we can discover that we've signed up for something that is simply not right, or find that things have changed, in a way that becomes unacceptable.

We should know our boundaries and be comfortable in them. Crossing that line is a recipe for disaster. If we're being pulled beyond them too often, it may be time to move on.

It's a good idea to check ourselves out, regularly, for the tangible impacts of what we're doing. Numbers, process and safety are all real considerations, and can easily be monitored. Remember, avoiding the check is actually worse than getting a bad result. We can usually do something to improve a bad result, but ignorance can kill.

Right-minded perceptions

Our right mind thrives on the shape of things and relationships. That's OK, we can still apply a little right-minded evaluation to the mix. Our right mind perceptions may feel a little more subjective but they're no less important for that.

Let's kick off with a basic happiness check:

Are we happy doing what we're doing?

Our activity may be a duty but it can also be a pleasure. If we get caught in a cycle of continual drudgery, where there is little or no joy, we won't last long. Our happiness, our wellbeing and our productivity will tail off, and end up in negative territory. Never underestimate the importance of a simple word like happiness.

Only we can define it, and measure it, in our own terms. We may be happy, but do we love what we're doing? We may even love the job, but hate the tasks. We often overlook the minutia of the job because, overall, it's something we've always wanted to do. Then, over time, the minutia mounts up.

Suddenly we're hating what we're actually doing, but have lost the ability to see it. We've become wrapped up in the romance of the job's label and become blind to its reality. When that happens, burn-out or crashing isn't far behind. A love-hate relationship is doomed to fail.

It's too easy to get swept up in the hurly burly of the moment. We go along for the ride, and we get a real buzz out of being hectic, or busy doing stuff. The bustle makes us feel important and the adrenalin makes us crave more and more action. The ride may be fun at the time, but we need to consider if it's fun that we're after.

If we're 'living to work', that's fine, but it might not last. If we're 'working to live', is the thrill-seeking actually distracting us from our real lives. There's a fine line between busy and addicted.

What's more, when we're in the same place, doing the same things for some time, we develop a sense of it being our duty to keep on going. We believe that people, and processes, depend on us and that we couldn't possibly move. We might even begin to believe that we're indispensable.

In truth, nobody is indispensable. So there's no need to have an undue sense of loyalty or obligation. Free will is more enduring than obligation. It's good to test whether we're still here because we want to be, or out of a sense of duty.

People make the world go round, they say. The people around us can make or break any situation.

They can support and encourage, or be our worst nightmare, pulling us down with constant nit-picking and criticism. It might be that the whole place feels toxic, or it might just be one specific person. Certainly, there's no benefit in tolerating the bad behaviour of others.

The interaction with others can be transactional or relationship based. If we're working a simple process with clear hand-offs, then a set of simple transactions will be perfectly good. If we need to be more collaborative, or we need to be more involved with each other, then we need to develop relationships. This includes, listening, sharing, suggesting and assisting each other - the need, and willingness, to relate needs to be mutual, to be effective. So check out how others are relating to us and whether that's enough for our needs.

With any group of people, egos are everywhere in their relationships. There's our own ego, which drives us to ambition and achievement, or to pride and over-reaching. Sadly, that can often drive us right over a cliff. We can end up alienating everyone around us, or burning ourselves out by grabbing for more than we can handle.

Other people's egos can also become overbearing on us. Their ambitions and self-importance can easily leave us feeling less valuable than we are.

That can then slip into a clash of egos, where it becomes a contest of wills and self-importance.

Those conflicts never end well and someone inevitably loses. Aiming for win-win is always a better outcome if we can achieve it. If it remains a battle, it might be time to back away gracefully.

We all love a good soap opera, but we don't necessarily want to live in one.

So many situations are unnecessarily turbulent and we do well to steer clear of the drama. The archetypal case is with a crisis manager boss. They love a crisis and will actively allow crises to emerge - for them, fixing 'problems' is a buzz, and feels easier to manage than smooth running.

Resources, deadlines, scope, quality or simple gossip are all great ways to generate a crisis. If the emotional temperature is constantly being cranked up, it may be time do ourselves a favour and to look for a cooler climate.

It all boils down to basic questions of honesty and trust. Those are difficult to build, but easy to break, and they'll show up in our behaviour and that of others.

It's great when we've learned to rely on the predictability of others words and actions; when they deliver, on time, every time, we get a sense of confidence and security. Even if they're consistently unreliable, at least we know where we stand and that we can't rely upon them.

It's easy to look back and judge if people are being trustworthy or not. The worst situation is where everything is constantly in flux and nothing can be relied upon. Spot the honesty and trust it where you can. If it's not there, it may be a deal breaker. We should be checking in regularly with the people around us. If people are ruining our wellbeing, we need to make it better, or consider our options to move out.

Finally, let's consider 'when' is our mind sitting. Now is now and the past has gone.

Often we can catch ourselves spending more and more time thinking about 'how it was before'. We find ourselves jumping out of our present situation and off to a time when everything felt better. Or we may be casting forward to a time when it will all be better. We try to convince ourselves that things will change and it'll be OK then.

Any of those feelings probably mean that we're unhappy with how it is today and that we're fantasising about another time. Now is all we really have, and today should be satisfying us, right now. Check out how often we find ourselves daydreaming about the past or the future, rather than now.

So, are we happy, right here, right now, with the people around us? If yes, we can carry on; if not, it might be time to move on.

Centre-minded perceptions

Our centre, or core, mind is mostly concerned with our deeper thoughts and beliefs. It is strongly driven by the unconscious areas of our minds. We often overlook it, because it seems somehow nebulous, unspecific or less disciplined.

Nevertheless, it's often our core beliefs that are our strongest drivers for staying or going from any situation. It's worthwhile to explore those factors, as objectively as we can, by being honest with ourselves about what really matters to us.

Our principle goals in life, and our purpose, lie at the very heart of whatever we are doing, or at least, they should. Our most satisfying times come from working on the things that we believe we were put on this earth to accomplish. It may be about our family and our heritage, and preserving a sense of continuity down the generations. It may be about personal learning, or teaching others and extending the wisdom of the world. Or it may be the job we're actually doing.

Many of the world's great people simply know that they were born to be doing what they are doing; a healer of some kind, a builder or engineer, or a dancer.

Whatever it may be, we can be sure that, when we're not 'on purpose', our lives will feel hollow and of less value to ourselves and to others. Being clear about our purpose, and working towards it, will fulfil us and sweep away any thoughts of quitting.

> "I was given such a great gift. It's a miracle that never stops amazing me and reminding me to give thanks, every day."
>
> **Jake Owen**
> **Country music singer**

Closely aligned with purpose will be our personal values in life. Here we're thinking about those fundamental aspects of our lives that we need to have in place for our peace of mind and overall wellbeing.

Our values could include some external attributes - like comfort, safety or financial security, and how we engage with the physical world. We may add more social elements like friendship, collaboration and connectedness. In short, how we engage with others.

Then there are the more internal values - like integrity, honesty, joy and learning. See the listing of 500 possible values in the downloadable Resilience Workbook for some ideas.

Sometimes it can be very difficult to be clear about what our values actually are, and they can also change over time, as we mature. If we begin to feel uneasy about our situation, and have an ill-defined urge to quit, it's likely that some of our core values are being violated, in some way. Understanding our values will help clarify the unease and help us to make more meaningful decisions.

Our centre mind is also concerned about balance. One of the most important areas to strike a good balance is between our work and the rest of our lives, simply because we spend so much of our lives at our work.

It's great when we get deep fulfilment from our work, but it's important to remember that life was not designed to be all work. The old adage 'All work and no play makes Jack a dull boy' has been true throughout the centuries and is never less so in our demanding modern times.

"The challenge of work-life balance is without question one of the most significant struggles faced by modern man."

Stephen Covey
Author, businessman

If we get our work and life out of balance, our core minds will begin to object, and drive us to uncharacteristic behaviour, until we right the balance. Again, we might need to look for what's missing, rather than for what's right in front of us, to find the balance that makes us happy.

Self-determination and personal freedom are part of what it means to be an individual. If we are too constrained by our situation, we'll begin to feel trapped in our lives, rather than living in them.

The term 'empowerment' has appeared recently and I see it as a sure sign that someone, somewhere, has recognised that they have tied us up with too many constraints. Watch out for the word and question the ways in which we might be disempowered.

Bundled into 'empowerment' are the notions of having a voice and being heard. This is not about the physical act of talking, but of knowing that what we have to say is important, and is being heard.

Having an audience for our insights makes us feel included and involved. Being listened to and heard validates us as individuals and may even give us feedback on what we are thinking. Even uncomfortable feedback is rewarding, because it gives us pause to rethink and learn. The worst case is where nobody listens to us.

When we go unheard, we can begin to feel isolated and unvalued, and feel like retreating from life. When we take the thought, patience and consideration to listen to others positively, then we are more likely to be heard positively by others. As a result, we will strengthen bonds, feel valued and deepen our sense of belonging – and so will the other people that we interact with.

So listen to others and be heard to build a sense of belonging.

Being grounded has entered our modern vocabulary, over the past couple of decades. It points to a general sense of being connected to our own selves and to our centre minds.

We're often so busy, doing things, that we forget to run the basic checks on how well those things suit us.

Being grounded is simply having the ability to know what matters to us, and being able to call it out, clearly and explicitly. 'New Age' techniques, like yoga and meditation, have become fashionable, and are simply ways of taking time to explore our inner mind space, and to rediscover our own important truths.

I'm a great believer in having some kind of mindfulness practice, to learn how to settle our minds and allow our truths to emerge. It might be through yoga or meditation, or other people might paint, listen to music, go for a walk, write poetry or simply write a journal at the end of each day. Whatever we do, we should always take the time to check in with our core selves, and be clear about whether what we're doing is a good fit.

This brings us, finally, to stability. Our centre mind is always comparing our current experiences with all those that have gone before. It remembers every moment that we've experienced, and judges everything as good or bad, safe or dangerous, pleasurable or hateful. Very often, our centre-mind will be calling out to us that something's not right, and we end up with that very unspecific uneasiness.

The most successful way to avoid, and quell, that uneasiness is to seek stability in our lives.

We're not talking about gridlock, or lack of advancement. Instead, we should be looking to draw from the lessons of our history, and do more of the things that reward and fulfil us, while doing less of what causes us trouble and concern.

Purpose, passion, values, connectedness and being grounded can all contribute to our stability, as we move forward in our grand schemes and our daily business. When, and if, the instability mounts to a level that we can't control, it may well be time to move to a more stable place and life.

We've seen that there are many drivers which can lead to us feeling like we want to quit, run away or simply be anywhere but here. By understanding how we perceive the world, in three different ways, we can begin to diagnose what's not sitting well with us.

In most situations, perception becomes reality, and we can change our reality simply by reframing our perceptions. This chapter has laid out the three principle mind frames (left, right and centre) and many of the aspects within them.

Using these frames can help us to review how we see the world around us and help us to feel more comfortable with it. What's more, it can help us identify some of the specific things that might be out of order. That will give us some areas to work on, and improve.

Of course, if the reframing still points up a bad situation then it really is time to move up and out. At least now we'll know why we're moving and what else we're looking for.

Clear decisions to move are not wrong, but sometimes we can bounce ourselves into hasty actions that are not based on clear-minded understanding.

So, by all means, let's change if we need to, but let's never quit.

Remember to download your free

Resilience

Workbook

Just follow the link below.

http://mikegordonbooks.com/download-siq-workbook/

You'll need the password that you find, at the end of Chapter 12

CHAPTER 8: BAD DAY AT WORK

"When you're having a bad day at work, a lot of times it's your head. When you're having good days, a lot of times it's the absence of the mind."

Curt Schilling
US major league baseball player

Nothing is perfect.

Even the best times can fall off the tracks and we end up having a bad day. It can happen at work, at home or anywhere else. There are simply days when nothing seems to go right - we've all had them.

Often, that's when a sense of hopelessness can creep in and we start to consider our options.

Is it time to jump ship? Is it time to quit?

Well, probably not.

In reality, one bad day does not make for a bad life. It's probably just a blip in an otherwise smooth line.

Before we go chucking everything up, it's probably wise to take a step back and get things into perspective. In this chapter we'll look at some tactics for coping with that bad day at work.

"No-one really has a bad life. Not even a bad day. Just bad moments."

Regina Brett
New York Times best-selling author

Most bad days start right at the beginning. If we get a false start to the day, it can very easily go downhill, all the way from there. At work, a bad day often begins before we even get there: we've overslept, the kids won't get ready; the train is late. And then the rest of the day just seems to get progressively worse.

Little mishaps, early in the morning, can easily throw us off balance and spark a spiral of negative thinking.

That negativity can follow us about and begin to infect everything around us. Eventually, we begin to hate the world and everything in it. We begin to see every tiny glitch as a sure sign of how awful the world is and we end up in a funk for the rest of the day.

But let's not panic. We know that we've got the whole day ahead of us, and it's pointless getting knocked down at the first hurdle. Yes it's a bummer, but what's happened has happened. Fretting about it can't make it un-happen. So, let's stop and take a breath.

My first tactic, when things start out badly, is to deal with the immediate situation right away. Then I take another breath. I reset the dials in my head and look forward to the rest of the day with as much composure as I can muster. There's great value in nipping negativity in the bud, before it gets a strong hold.

We can simply choose to have a better perspective if we look for opportunities and wins, instead of shortcomings and faults. We know that continuing in a negative frame of mind will only make us perform worse, and bad things will continue to happen.

By simply pausing for a moment we can usually overcome the mishap and make a fresh start. Remember, we're normally the high-value superstar that everyone appreciates, and one little glitch doesn't suddenly turn us into failures. There's no need to make a bad incident become a bad day. Getting off on the wrong foot is no reason to step off the path altogether.

"Positive anything is better than negative nothing."

Elbert Hubbard,
American writer, publisher, artist, and philosopher (1856-1915)

I used to hate mornings. I'd drag myself out of bed and wander about in a trance for half-an-hour or more. Coffee, shower and out. No wonder I had so many bad days. I never took the time, or care, to set myself up for a good day. Little wonder I didn't have them.

Nowadays I have a morning ritual that helps set me up for a good day, not a bad one.

Firstly, I've had enough sleep. I knew what the day ahead was likely to bring and I've made sure that I've had enough quality sleep, the night before, to tackle it. We're simply kidding ourselves if we believe that we can go to bed, tired-out and late, and expect to have a stellar day in the morning. It will be worse still, if we go to bed full of food or alcohol.

Our bodies are finely-tuned machines that need some nurturing and maintenance to keep them running well. Resources get depleted and parts get tired and worn out. So rest and nutrition are the prerequisites for a good day, at work or wherever. Oddly enough, we all acknowledge that this makes good sense, yet still we gamble that we'll be OK. Burnout won't happen to us. Well, let's wise up. Nobody is super-human.

My good day really gets started before I even get out of bed. Wrapped up in a warm bed is a great time to consider what the day ahead will bring. It's a great time to set our intentions for the day.

Notice I'm saying intentions, not plans. We've only just come out of sleep and our minds aren't yet laser sharp or focused. It's the time for a more visionary and emotional sense check; settling how we want our day to be, more than what's going to happen in it. Focus positively on the big picture vison for the day, not the minutiae. I don't get out of bed until I know why I'm doing it.

Some people like to meditate first thing in the morning and I am a strong advocate of meditation at any time. This just happens to be my form of morning meditation. Wrapped up, warm, horizontal... and comfortable. I see no need to change my position just because I'm resetting my mind. Then I get out of bed in a positive frame of mind.

And while I'm on the subject of getting out of bed, here's another great tip. Make the bed.

Having a well-made and inviting bed to climb into at night is a joy at the end of a long day. So, get up and pull the covers back and let the bed air a little. Then have a shower. When we're done showering, go back and make the bed. We can even do it naked. Why not? Let the air circulate around us as we cool off. It's a simple routine that will pay us back later. Make it part of our morning ritual.

I then set about the rest of my morning rituals; breakfast, brushing teeth, dressing, arranging the day's tools and admin. It's a well-trodden path and requires little thought.

I go through those motions on autopilot, while my mind is deepening and crystallising how the rest of my day will shape up.

For that to happen, I've already plotted how those rituals will go. They have become routine and I try, as much as possible, to clear any encumbrances from their smooth execution. There is soap and shampoo in the shower, milk in the fridge, no toys scattered around the floor. Clothes are ironed, papers are in order and keys are on the hook by the door. In other words, a good day has started with a little organisation the evening before. Autopilot can be engaged from the outset.

Just like a good morning routine, there's great value in a good evening routine, too. No matter how tired we are by the end of the day, it always pays to have a well-ordered home when we get up next day.

Take a few moments to clear up a little. Make sure there's everything we'll need for the next day so that we have a clear run in the morning. If there's no milk in the fridge, let's understand that we're going to have a scented tea and some toast in the morning rather than the usual milky coffee and cereal. It's a tiny act of acceptance rather than going to bed with resentment.

I make notes in my journal every evening; switch off the TV or music and take about 10 minutes to jot down all of my achievements from that day, recalling all of the events, the tiny victories and pleasures, that came my way. Even the bad things have a lesson of some sort, so they also get written down with a positive spin. It's all about going to bed with a feeling of contented gratitude for the day just past, of falling asleep in a positive frame of mind. It works wonders.

I'm fortunate enough to work at home and the commute is just a few steps downstairs to my study. But even then, I dress for work. It's all part of the mind-setting. For those of us who need to commute to work, just think how much better it would be if we left the house each morning in a positive frame of mind and everything we needed was in place. It sets us up for a good day, every day

"Optimism is the faith that leads to achievement. Nothing can be done without hope and confidence."

Helen Keller
American author, political activist (1880-1968)

It's true, some days really are bad, even if we have the best intentions and routines. Some days really can be the worst day of our life: death of a loved one, being fired, our home burning down, are just a few extreme examples.

Instances like that need all of our resilience. But, most likely, what we would usually describe as a bad day is nothing like that. No, it's probably more about the mounting levels of minutia piling up and making us want to give up; or the nagging boss who's on our case; or losing the deal that we've been fighting for.

So, without dismissing the possiblity of catastrophes, we can make the distinction between those truly traumatic events and a regular day, good, bad or indifferent. Keep a sense of perspective: are we having a catastrophic day, or simply a bad day?

Let's save our energies for the really bad ones and learn to deal with the normal bad days more successfully. And it starts with that simple reality check.

Inevitably, the odd bad day will still crop up, and we need to know how to handle it with equanimity. There's no need to make a bad day worse.

A bad day is a great time to believe the unbelievable.

As we wipe away the poop the bird of fortune has dropped on us, we can start by looking beyond the present situation. Although it doesn't feel like it right then, we know that this too will pass.

Things will come good again. Simply cast our minds forward to the time when it'll be back to smooth running.

If we unhook from the 'now' for a moment, we can imagine the good times to come. See the pot of gold ahead.

This is not an invitation to dramatise all of the bad things that might happen from this bad situation. Life really is a pot of gold, not the proverbial crock of you-know-what. When we believe in a good future, it's more likely to happen.

> ## "If you have a bad day in baseball and start thinking about it, you will have 10 more."
>
> **Sammy Sosa**
> **Major league baseball player**

It's also a great time to look back. Let's remember how good we are. We can all recognise that we've had mishaps and sticky situations before... and we're still here: We didn't get fired, we didn't quit and nobody died.

No, we coped with that bad day and we carried on. What's more we've learned from those previous bad days. We took note of what happened last time around and how we managed to get through it. We even wrote about those bad days in our journal (see, there is a subtle plan working here).

We've looked at the actions we did then, and we've packaged them up as resilience, for a day such as this. That's right, we can see the pattern of recoveries from the past and turn them into our system for a bad day. Simply open up the 'bad day resilience package', take a sip of our own medicine and work our own system to take command of a bad day and turn it around.

This is exactly the time to stay away from the dramas. It's not the time to seek out the 'misery club'. We all know who they are; those folk who hang around and wail about how terrible it all is. Maybe it's in the coffee room, around the photocopier or even outside in the yard. Let's give those folk a wide berth right now.

"There's nothing wrong or evil about having a bad day. There's everything wrong with making others have to have it with you."

Neil Cavuto
US TV anchor and commentator

If we're already feeling at a low ebb, the last thing we need is to indulge in a pity party with others. Misery loves company, so why would we seek it out and offer ourselves up to it? Instead, let's be grateful for what we've got. Enjoy what life brings us, even if it's a bad day today.

This includes appreciating what we have, beyond work (friends, family or home). It will put this bad situation into better perspective and help to turn it around. We have a life beyond this bad moment.

If it's in work, we're probably living our passion; if it's away from the job, we know why we're there, right now, even on that bad day. A little perspective will help us talk more positively about life and a better vibe will emerge. Faced with our overall radiance, the misery makers will fade away. That's why I advocate having a journal and writing only positive words; gratitude and lessons learnt. Remember the good times and be grateful for even the bad days.

Smile, shrug and laugh. It's not just an old wives' tale that *'laughter is the best medicine'* - it really does help us change our perspective.

The physical act of smiling and laughing out loud causes chemical changes in our brain (all those delicious endorphins) and shifts our minds to a better place.

It might sound mad, but I used to hold a pencil sideways between my teeth and gently stretch my mouth into a fake smile. It felt so silly that, within seconds, I'd have a real smile and things didn't seem so bad. Nowadays, I know where my happy place is and I can tap into it at will. Disasters can happen, yet I can still muster a positive attitude by simply thinking of a good time and painting on a smile. Try it, it works!

Or if nobody's around, just sit at the desk and chuckle. As a last resort, I've sent individuals into the supplies room, or out to the street to laugh it out. You'll be amazed how quickly a bad day at work can be turned around simply by deciding not to take it too seriously.

Of course, not everyone is a paid-up member of the pity party. There will be plenty of people around from whom we can seek support and solace. It's never a bad thing to get up, find a friend or colleague and laugh it out. No need to make it a tale of catastrophe, simply describe the ridiculousness of it all.

We should never be afraid to seek help. It's OK to consider if we need some external support. Friends, colleagues and family have all had bad days, too, and might be able to lend a listening ear or share some practical advice about what helps them cope.

Those other people probably can't fix the problem itself but talking it out will clear our minds and motivate us to positive action.

In extreme cases, it might even be time to seek help from a professional coach or therapist. If it is a workplace-related issue, perhaps the organisation has an employee assistance programme that can be consulted and can offer advice?

I've seen some remarkable turnarounds in clients in my own coaching work. It all begins with awareness of the situation and accepting that even bad situations can be turned around, so that they begin to look more hopeful and become easier to bear.

Whatever else, it's important to remember that we are not in this alone. Recognising our limits, and reaching out, will often make things better, just with that simple action.

"There is nothing either good or bad but thinking makes it so."

William Shakespeare
Poet, playwright (1564-1616)

On the practical side, if things aren't working well today, that's OK. Simply change it a little. There are often opportunities in the day to change the little tasks at hand. Swapping tasks will usually break the downward cycle and get us succeeding again.

Depending on our jobs, the change may only be for 10 minutes, or it could be the whole day. If that document is driving us nuts, move on to a spreadsheet. If the books won't balance, do some invoicing.

In extreme cases, do something simple and mundane: I catch up on my shredding, put away that pile of files or call a client and set up a lunch. We all have lots of opportunities to turn a bad day around by catching ourselves doing something right. Success breeds success and we'll soon find our attitudes shifting.

What if the bad days are becoming more frequent? It might be something more systemic in our job overall. Most people can find a way to add a little variety or freshness to what they do. Can we add something to our routine or change the pattern? How about learning a new skill, changing the process, brainstorming new ideas with friends and colleagues or justifying a new project to the boss?

All of these can make a material change to our work, and will certainly give us a better sense of control in our situation. It's always best if we can take control of that bad day and take steps to stop it from coming back, again and again.

With a more positive attitude in place, good things will begin to happen once again.

Yet sometimes, even after trying the tactics of surviving a bad day at work, we realise that it simply isn't working for us any longer. It really is too much. The bad days are coming around too often and it truly is time to move on.

Even then, it's important to step back and consider carefully, before moving forward.

In the next chapter we'll be looking at the signs that the job really isn't right for us.

In the meantime, we don't need to make a bad day worse. The last thing that we need to do is to jeopardise the status quo. We need to live through the short term, to get to the long term.

So, even if we are getting ready to move on, we'll probably want a smooth transition.

It's important to maintain a positive mental attitude towards ourselves, our work, our colleagues and our bosses.

A bad day at work (or even bad days) is no reason to ruin our prestige and reputation, in the short term.

We need to hang in there and maintain good opinions throughout. Keep smiling and share whatever joy we still have.

It's never a good idea to close our eyes and simply jump into the unknown. Our bad day at work will be made more tolerable when we have a plan and begin putting it into action.

"Nothing in this world can take the place of persistence.

Talent will not: nothing is more common than unsuccessful men with talent.

Genius will not; unrewarded genius is almost a proverb.

Education will not: the world is full of educated derelicts.

Persistence and determination alone are omnipotent."

Calvin Coolidge
President of the United States (1923-1929)

Once again, we need to step back and develop a strategy. We need to be realistic about how long it might take, to reconsider what we actually want to do next and where we might find it.

Remember, changing to something new is not quitting. Each change is an opportunity to renew or reinvent.

Maybe more of the same, in a different place, isn't what we need this time around. Maybe this is the time to shift the pattern altogether.

I've helped many clients plan their transition, and I'm always pleasantly surprised by how much better they feel, just by working on a plan.

In fact, I've even had a couple of clients who have decided to stay put. Merely having worked out a plan, or an alternative, has been enough to make the present situation workable.

In short, there is no benefit in allowing a bad day at work to bounce us into a knee-jerk reaction. We should always think it through: plan the move, and move through the plan.

In the meantime, what does our 'bad day resilience package' look like?

Have we recorded our good and bad days? Do we know how we've dealt with bad days in the past. Do we have a clear sense of how things turn around after a bad day?

No? Then perhaps it's time to start a journal as part of our evening routine.

Develop the habit of documenting our good and bad days and how they turned out. Its amazing how powerful a journal can be as a learning resource.

It builds resilience and gives us ideas on how to deal with those bad days when they crop up next time.

So, start journalling... with purpose.

Remember to download your free

Resilience

Workbook

Just follow the link below.

http://mikegordonbooks.com/download-siq-workbook/

You'll need the password that you find, at the end of Chapter 12

CHAPTER 9: WHEN ENOUGH IS ENOUGH

> "Work? I never worked a day in my life. I always loved what I was doing, had a passion for it."
>
> **Ernie Banks**
> **Baseball player, Chicago Cubs**

For most of us, going to work is an inescapable part of life. Whether it's a paid job, or unpaid responsibilities, we are obliged to turn up and be productive. Sometimes, it can feel like too much and we begin to think about quitting. We reach the point where enough is enough.

What's more, our motivations for being there are rarely the issue, and it's more a question of how we see the job that we're doing, in the moment we're doing it. Regardless of the job itself, it can often feel like it's simply too much.

That's probably a good point to stop and consider why we might be hating our job, and what has lead us to thoughts of quitting, or at least changing for something else. Is it the job that we hate, or what the job means to us? Has the job changed to become unacceptable, or have we changed in some way?

Entrepreneurs, and other successful business people, elite athletes and artists, often go to work because it's part of their life's purpose, their passion. We can think of these as the 'live to work' people. They have an overriding purpose that spurs them to great things and they are dedicated to what they do.

Even for this type of person there is a danger that their passion becomes an obsession. They're driven by their passion, and forget to take stock of the price that they are paying, to reach their goals. Then, one day it all becomes too much, they feel burned out and the passion becomes overwhelmed by reality.

I'm reminded of the opening scene of Puccini's opera, La Boehme. It begins in a garret, where a group of young artists and writers are huddled around a sparse fire, trying to stay warm. Things have become so wretched that they have begun to burn the furniture, as well as their art works and manuscripts, to keep the fire going. We meet them in a life-or-death conflict between their ideals and the practicality of staying alive. Of course, being opera, the heroine eventually loses the struggle and dies. It is a romantic tragedy, after all!

Muhammad Ali had always been a larger-than-life character. He reached the highest pinnacle of his industry - he became undisputed heavyweight boxing champion of the world.

His philosophy at that time was remarkably simple.

"It's just a job. Grass grows, birds fly, waves pound the sand. I beat people up."

Muhammad Ali
Former world heavyweight boxing champion

Sadly, in retrospect, we have seen the price that he paid for reaching the top. Ali had been diagnosed variously as suffering from *dementia pugilistica*, a form of trauma-induced dementia, or *pugilistic parkinsonism*, trauma-induced Parkinson's disease. The exact diagnosis is still debated but even he recognised the reality of the situation:-

> **"I've been in the boxing ring for 30 years and I've taken a lot of punches, so there is a great possibility something could be wrong."**

Muhammad Ali
Former world heavyweight boxing champion

I'm not suggesting, for a moment, that we live in a romantic tragedy or that we will ever be elite athletes, stretching our bodies beyond their limits.

Nevertheless, I do see many go-getters failing to recognise the signs that their passion is spilling over into obsession. We can all benefit from a moment to review whether the prize is worth the cost.

I have seen many clients from the service or caring professions. They've dedicated their lives to helping and supporting others. By the time they come to me, seeking help, it's usually because they've forgotten to care for themselves. They've suppressed their own needs for the needs of others. They've lost their sense of priority for nurturing themselves, and for having a life beyond their profession.

Their vocational passion has become all-consuming, either through choice or neglect.

All too often, I meet these clients when they have developed an overbearing sense of guilt or shame about needing to re-set their balance. They believe that they couldn't possibly step back a little, because it would be abandoning the people that they care for. They consider that the needs of others outweigh their own needs.

"I don't like saying 'no' to people, and I'm going to have to learn how to say 'no' more."

Eric Betzig
Nobel Prize winner (Chemistry, 2014)

There is a strong need for them to step back and reconsider; to put themselves back in the centre of their own life. It's a case of providing the best care to others by being the best version of themselves in life. A great mantra for carers is to recognise that

Self-nurture is not selfishness.

Then there are those we can consider to be the 'work to live' people. Typically, they'll be employees in an organisation, or members of partnerships, where risk and workload are shared with other people. They'll tell us that they are working to earn money to do other things outside work.

When their life is in balance, they'll have a happy and active life away from work. They get to work on time, with a smile on their face for what the day will bring. Then they'll leave work on time, still with a smile in anticipation of what's yet to come.

They are working to live and content to be at work because of what else it enables. I suspect the majority of the working population would consider themselves to be in the 'work to live' category. It's also where a majority of my clients sit.

By the time that I see them, they will be looking for guidance on how to get their life back. They'll complain about being 'cash rich, time poor'. They're working so hard to earn money, that it has begun to consume their free time. They'll tell me that there are simply not enough hours in the day. They've got the money but no time to spend it.

"People are chasing cash, not happiness. When you chase money, you're going to lose. You're just going to. Even if you get the money, you're not going to be happy."

Gary Vaynerchuk
Entrepreneur, investor, author

They'll often spend their money on more and more extravagant gifts to themselves. It might be a fast car, a flashy watch, a big house, or the best brands at home and about their person.

Labels matter to them. Bigger is better; more is more. In most cases, they're looking for answers outside of themselves, rather than being clear about the relative balance of the things that they value.

I'll often ask these people which they'd rather have, an hour with the family or another hour at work.

I'm often surprised at the shock they feel at the question and at their own answer. Of course it would be their family, but the idea has escaped them somewhere along the line.

A good mantra in those cases might be

Life is for living, not consuming.

Whether we're in the 'live to work' category or the 'work to live' group, we all have a responsibility to check out our work/life balance.

When we begin to feel stressed, or anxious about our work, it's probably a good time to step back, set priorities and lay down some boundaries. It's the time to remember what having a life means to us.

Even the best job in the world can become the job we hate, if we don't take time look after the basics. But all is not lost; every situation is recoverable. There are a few simple ideas that can keep us motivated at whatever we're doing.

So let's take some time to take stock of our situation, and ask ourselves some fundamental questions.

Check alignment

First, let's look at ourselves in the context of the job we're doing. We've been in the job for a while, and it's simply not what we expected. The company's values, or method of operation, are not what we expected. Simply put, are we out of whack with the demands of the job at hand?

How often have we heard friends tell us the job isn't what it promised? Or that the employer sold them a rosy picture of how it would be. But is it really the employer's fault alone? They want to hire good employees and will turn on the charm to win our engagement. And that's a two-way street.

When we're looking for a new job, it's very easy to hear what we want to hear. Often, we're desperate for change, and the urge to move clouds our judgment.

Our prospective employer may have been perfectly clear about what the firm stands for and what the job entails. But were we listening?

From our perspective, recruitment interviews are a process to bring us the choice of whether to accept an offer or not. Of course, we're trying to get that offer from the prospective employer. Our strategy should be to present enough of ourselves to be offered the job.

Equally, it should include gathering enough evidence to make an informed decision. It's great to be offered the job, but we need to be clear about our walk-away criteria. It's not just about money; it includes the 'look and feel' of the job, too. In other words, what it entails in reality.

So, if the job doesn't match up to expectations, is it the job, or our expectations that are off? We should always be prepared to walk away if the job doesn't suit us, even before we start.

Spot the change

Then again, perhaps the job really has changed, in some fundamental way, from when we started out.

If it has, then what has changed? Are the changes acceptable to us, and would we have chosen to take the job, at the outset, if those changes were already in place?

That's where our walk-away criteria are so important.

Good jobs do change, over time, and the definition of 'good' lies squarely with us. Can we accept, and live with, the changes, or has the job become something materially different to our needs and wants? Only we can decide that.

Or it might be exactly what it promised, but somehow we find that, in reality, it doesn't sit well with our own values.

Maybe we've changed?

Perhaps our needs have matured and outstripped our job's ability to deliver what we want. It's essential that we know why we're doing the job, and that we check that it continues to give us what we want.

Douglas Coupland, the Canadian novelist and artist, seems to have been clear about what he wanted.

"I've had maybe 20 jobs, big and small, and I've never hated any of them. At the same time, the moment the learning curve flattened, I was out of there."

Douglas Coupland
Canadian Novelist and Artist

In any of these cases, we can end up feeling like our values are being violated, and we are simply not being satisfied at work. That's the perfect recipe for creating the job we hate. That's the time to take a long hard look at our values, in practice, and how they fit within the working context.

A slight mismatch on peripheral issues may be bearable and we can carry on. But what if they go to the core of our being?

Is there a fundamental deal-breaker, between our mutual expectations?

Whatever we do, we need to strike a realistic balance between acceptable and unacceptable. Often a simple discussion, and adjustment, can turn things around and the job we hate can become pretty good.

Stay balanced

Every job carries obligations, responsibilities and workload. Some loading is a good thing and can be used as a challenge to get us up and going, however, too much can lead to stress, and a sense of overbearing pressure.

So are we being challenged, or is it pressure?

Challenge engages us, lifts us up and mobilises us; it's a positive internal response to an external stimulus. We choose to accept it and respond positively to it. For many, challenge is a strong motivator and a power for progress.

"Courage is grace under pressure."

Ernest Hemingway
American novelist, short story writer, journalist

Pressure lies heavily on us and weighs us down. It's a negative, internal response to external stimuli, which drags us down, demotivates us, and makes us stall. Typically, we see pressure as an obligation that we are forced to accept, rather than something we would necessarily choose.

It's very easy for challenges to mount up, if we let them. We can slip into a responsive mode of taking all comers; accepting and stepping up to every challenge, often without thinking. That's how pressure can build and burn-out isn't far behind.

Things we used to love have become chores and burdens. In all probability, self-determination has vanished under the mass of imposed duty. The dream job has become the job that we hate.

So what's changed? Perhaps it's the nature of the job itself or simply the sheer volume of demands, which have increased beyond an acceptable level.

When the job content has changed, to a point where we're doing stuff that we just don't want to do, why not speak to our boss or supervisor and find out if there is more engaging work that we can take on. In other words, we can fix the problem by changing the job.

Or maybe it's us who have changed. We can simply become bored with the same old stuff, day after day. What used to energise us has simply become humdrum and dull. If so, we can look for ways to switch it up a little.

Ask to swap tasks with co-workers. Seek a change to a new role. Volunteer for additional duties to involve us in something new and interesting. It's amazing how flexible employers can be when we go, with a positive frame of mind, and suggest making our jobs more engaging. After all, we have been valuable to them until now and it's in their interests to keep us motivated and productive.

Two-way appreciation

There's the old saying, 'A thank you costs nothing'. Showing a little appreciation, to and from co-workers, goes a long way to making us feel involved. So are we being appreciated? And are we appreciating their appreciation?

"I always concentrate on respecting human beings and their lives and the meaning within their lives, and I believe that is something people around the world can appreciate."

Kim Ki-duk
South Korean filmmaker

I'm amazed at how difficult we find it to accept compliments and praise, or even a simple *'thanks'* from others. We bluster and deflect appreciation with responses like *'I was only doing my job'* or *'It was nothing'*.

English, German, Dutch, French, Spanish, and many more languages, have an automatic *'It was nothing'* response to a simple *'Thank you'*. Well, frankly, it wasn't 'nothing'; not to us. We are expressing gratitude for something that matters to us. Dismissing it effectively dismisses the value that we feel for the gift they have just given us. So let's accept gratitude with grace. And let's say *'thank you'* and mean it.

American culture has recognised the power of accepting gratitude and has evolved into the obligatory *'You're welcome'* when anyone says *'Thank you'*.

When heartfelt, *'you're welcome'* can create a fleeting moment of bonding and mutual respect. All too often, however, it's simply a reflex action and has little meaning.

I do advocate showing gratitude with a *'Thank you'* but I always try to add in the reason why I'm grateful. *'Thank you, that has saved me so much time.'* Or *'Thank you, this is so unexpected'* or *'Thank you, you've brightened my day'*.

Then, when people reply with *'You're welcome,'* they'll probably mean it more sincerely, because they understand the contribution that they've made.

Being genuine in our gratitude is more likely to elicit more genuine appreciation in return. So, before we get into a funk about feeling unappreciated for the gift of our efforts, we might need to take stock of our own behaviour.

First, do we show appreciation? Do we radiate thanks and gratitude to those around us? Appreciation is circular; we need to give it to get it, to learn the habit of being heartfelt with our thanks.

Second, do we deserve appreciation? Is our work up to scratch?

If we turn in lacklustre work, we can't expect to be appreciated for it. So let's raise the bar. Let's go a little beyond the basics and begin to shine. Then we'll see the appreciation flow.

Finally, when we've done a good job, there's no harm in acknowledging it to ourselves. Nobody likes a braggart, but simple self-appreciation is infectious. If we show ourselves the love, others will join in. Being justly proud of our work will highlight a good job, when we do it. Others will notice and appreciate. Overall, building up an atmosphere of appreciation can go a long way to turning the job that we hate into a 'great place to be'.

"Show me the money"

Next, we need to look at the thorny issue of money. We're turning out great work, and showing appreciation all around, but we don't believe that we're being paid enough. Pay is always a touchy subject, but it has one huge advantage over other concerns - it's objective.

It's really easy to identify just how much we've been paid for our labours. It'll be written down in clear numbers, either on a cheque or in a bank statement, or handed over in cash. It has the benefit of being precise.

Determining whether it's enough is more complicated.

Remember, working for money is an exchange of value - effort for money. Whether it's enough is a matter of our own perceptions. I'm amazed at how few people actually sit down and do the maths.

Too often we have a sense of what we're worth, rather than what the job's worth.

That's when emotions start to fly.

> **"A lot of people don't enjoy their job, they may even hate it, but I am lucky enough to be able to make a living through my passion."**
>
> **Martin Yan**
> **Chinese-American chef and food writer**

If our pay is out of line with our peers in the company, or across the industry, we have a case, to take to our bosses, for a raise.

If it's in line with our peers, and we still can't pay the bills, then perhaps we're in the wrong job after all, and need to find something more lucrative.

"I'm proud I've been able to pay my rent doing what I love."

Travie McCoy
American rapper, singer-songwriter

I'm constantly saddened by ongoing reports of pay inequality for women, people of colour, those who are disabled or even cases of discrimination related to sexual orientation.

It's as if just having a job, at all, carries a diversity tax for diverse employees.

I always advocate applying some kind of fairness test. If it's unfair, call it out. If the bosses refuse to adjust it to parity, then at least we know where we stand, and can make some informed decisions, rather than rely on purely subjective emotion.

If it's fairly balanced, but we still want more, we need to consider what we are doing differently, that makes our effort materially different. What tangible factors make us worth more?

When we clarify the hard numbers (input versus output), we can take the heat out of the discussion, and avoid it becoming a grudge match.

Demonstrate a difference and we can then count it up, in terms of added value, for added reward. Simply expecting more for ordinary output will get us nowhere, it will simply encourage growing resentment.

It's a sure recipe for turning a good job into the job we hate.

Look ahead

Our sense of advancing is another great motivator Take that away and we begin to feel trapped and pointless. Then, even the best job becomes a grind. As soon as there's a sense of our career being arrested, we begin to view today's job in a different light. Love can easily turn to hate.

Actually, it's not today's job that's become hateful, it's the future prospects. Well, here's the thing - the future hasn't happened yet. We have time to change our prospects; to change our future.

Another worrying trend in diversity issues centres on older workers. There's growing evidence to suggest that older workers are being frozen out of development and career advancement. Investment in training, and skills building, seems to be focused on younger and mid-career workers, while older workers are deemed to have all of the skills they need, without further investment.

But there is light on the horizon for older workers. As the population ages, so too does the talent pool. The more insightful employers are investing in re-training schemes, to keep their older workers engaged and productive. They recognise that experience has a value beyond mere effort.

It's not a universal realisation today, but commercial imperative has an odd habit of catching up with demographics, over time. Older workers, in return, have an obligation to stay flexible and to embrace change in their own jobs.

In Chapter Two we took a moment to explore dealing with a fork on the road, about working around obstacles and accepting new challenges. By thinking ahead, we can explore what we could be doing, that is more engaging, challenging and rewarding.

Of course, this also means that we need to be clear about what our new, or extra, value will be, that returns extra reward to us. Remember, it's an exchange of value.

When we have a vision of a better future, our current job can cease being a grind. What's more, the new opportunities will revive our passion and our feelings of appreciation. Who knows, we may even get a pay rise out of it.

"People often ask me whether I prefer theatre or film, and the answer is that I prefer the one I'm not doing: The grass is always greener."

Dame Helen Mirren
English actress, Academy Award winner

We can view Dame Helen's philosophy as one of mere wistfulness and discontentment. Instead, I see it as a measure of energetic pursuit of the next opportunity. Even while she is delivering a class performance in her current role, she is mindful that change is just around the corner and she's building excitement for that change. She is now in her 70s and shows no sign of stopping any time soon.

Over there?

Does the grass look greener on the other side? How often do we look outside our own situation and convince ourselves that other people are doing better than us? It's tempting to believe that others are living the dream, when we're not. But how often does their reality actually match our perceptions of them?

Answer, never! That's right... NEVER!

There's a simple reason why comparison with others is futile - they're not us. Even if they are blissfully happy where they are, there is no guarantee that we would be equally happy in their shoes. If fact, it's most likely that we wouldn't be, because their shoes simply wouldn't fit us.

We look at other people's houses, cars, families or jobs from our current perspective. It looks great from where we stand today. If we strive hard, and make big changes, we could end up where they are. But would it be the same? No, certainly not.

Wherever we go, we take ourselves, and our baggage, with us. Every situation is experienced through the lens of our own history and heritage. Our appreciation of a new situation will always be coloured by who we are, where we've been and what we had to do to get where we are.

"Be careful what you wish for, lest it come true."

Folk saying

If we've had to work extra hard to improve our situation, have we sacrificed too much of what we really value to get there?

I see many people who have worked hard for a promotion - to get more money, to have a better life. Then, when we look closer, they're now working longer hours, travelling away from home more, eating badly, sleeping less --and experiencing many other consequences of accepting greater stress. They've achieved the letter of the contract with themselves, but not the spirit. The bigger rewards have brought a higher price than expected.

So, when looking for a change to somewhere else, be clear about why we want it.

Is this something genuinely good for us, or is it simply that over there is not here? There's lots that we can do, to make our own lives better, which isn't simply acting out other people's playbook or script. We can, and should, write our own script.

Seek advice

We all have our gurus and mentors in life. The best ones encourage us to be reflective, to set our own goals, and to measure success against our own yardsticks. There are many people that I admire greatly, and whom I strive to emulate in some way. But I would never want to be just like them.

Instead, I take smaller lessons, from a wide spectrum of sources, and blend them into being the best me I can be. There is only one me and I want that uniqueness to define myself, not anyone else's idea of good or great. We can all learn from the 'greats' but we'll never, ever, be them.

"No one lives long enough to learn everything they need to learn starting from scratch. To be successful, we absolutely, positively have to find people who have already paid the price to learn the things that we need to learn to achieve our goals."

Brian Tracy
Author, motivational speaker

There are lessons we can learn from other people's experience. Rather than envy what other people have, or have achieved, I'd suggest it's better to learn from them, and adapt it for our own unique situation. We can watch what they did, and learn the lessons from it, not slavishly emulate the details of their processes or outcome. It's a question of changing ourselves, and letting the rewards flow to the value we deliver.

So, when we begin to feel that enough is enough, we can begin by asking 'enough of what?'. We've seen, repeatedly, that quitting in the absolute sense is not an option. Everything represents change and we can manage change safely.

Simply throwing everything up, and starting over from scratch, is a myth.

Even if we went into some kind of witness protection programme, with a new name, address, job and lifestyle, we'd never really be changing our identity. Our true identity. We can never leave ourselves behind.

If we are overwhelmed by our situation, or we're no longer feeling satisfied, it might well be time to change. But remember, life is like a river; it's continuous. It might turn corners, it might go underground, it might be fast or slow and it might even plunge over cliffs, but it's still the same river. If we're unhappy with any aspect of life, we are perfectly free to change it. In fact, we're the only ones who can. And that change starts here.

None of us gets a clean sheet, there are no do-overs for the life we've already had. Any new job or life starts from here. We can't simply wish that we had a better starting point.

This is it. Today is today. We are where we are and wishing it was different gets us nowhere.

In the following chapters we'll look at whether we should make the big changes, and how to do it safely. Before we go there, however, I suggest that we stay where we are, and do a little internal re-setting.

Let's be sure that our heads and hearts are in the right place, and that we're moving on for the best of reasons. Simply because 'it's not here' is a dangerous reason to want to be elsewhere.

There could be some physical and practical aspects to our lives, or jobs, that we don't like, but most of the reasons for disliking where we are will stem from our attitude to it. Most often, the job is perfectly fine but it's our feelings towards it that have changed.

What are our motivations, our values and our needs and wants? Are we clear about those and are we certain we can't make today's life fit us better? Are we really in the job that we hate, or are there things we can do to fix the here and now?

I've learned that we have more options available to us, in the roles we currently have, than we ever acknowledge.

Too often, we simply take the reality of our existence as presented, without question. Instead of looking for ways out of uncomfortable situations, let's look for ways through, or up, from them. Start by changing our mind-set to the current context and look for the plusses which we can build on. The minuses are the areas we can work on and resolve. Creativity and resilience are our best allies, when enough feels like enough.

Stay put, and work through the issues, before considering moving out.

Remember to download your free

Resilience

Workbook

Just follow the link below.

http://mikegordonbooks.com/download-siq-workbook/

You'll need the password that you find, at the end of Chapter 12

CHAPTER 10: TIME TO GO?

"It's time to say goodbye, but I think goodbyes are sad and I'd much rather say hello. Hello to a new adventure."

Ernie Harwell
American sports broadcaster

In earlier chapters, we've looked at ways of reviewing and building our path to resilience. We've invested considerable effort in looking at how we might make our present situation better, and more acceptable. But there does come a point when it really is time to move on. So let's leave wisely.

In the remaining chapters of this book we'll explore critical considerations that face us, once we have made that decision. But first we must look at some facts about major change and our mindset for leaving.

Let's recognise that change can be scary, and many of us put off making important changes, simply because we're uncertain or afraid.

The truth is that change happens to us all, either by choice or due to unforeseen circumstances. We may as well get used to the fact and see it as something positive. If we manage change well it can be a power for good, not evil, not only for us, but those around us.

Good things don't happen by accident when such a transition is under way. It's a straight choice between embracing change that we control, or enduring change that we don't.

Let's start with a few facts about big change in our lives.

"Successful people recognise crisis as a time for change - from lesser to greater, smaller to bigger."

Edwin Louis Cole
Founder, Christian Men's Network

At work, the average tenure in a job is four to five years (US Bureau of Labor Statistics, 2012). Over a 40-year career, we might change jobs between eight and ten times. Some of these moves might be voluntary (where we decide it's time to go), or involuntary (when change is forced upon us). Whichever it is, it's a pretty common event, and the concept of having a 'job for life' has well and truly gone.

Of course, personal circumstances will vary, and some people will stay in one place for decades, but the statistics do point to turbulence and change as the growing norm. And whenever we hear 'turbulence' we should be thinking 'resilience, flexibility and adaptability'. So, when it's time to go, it's worth working through that change carefully with positive intentions, resilience and adaptability.

It's also a question of how big the changes need to be. It might be a simple job transfer, or a complete shift in our career direction.

Oddly, I would suggest that the emotional trials and practical steps for any degree of change are broadly the same. It's simply the scale of change that will be different. Either way, every one of them is a break point in the status quo.

It's an opportunity to review how we're travelling and how well our current speed and direction are serving us. When it's time to go, we can gear up to simply change the job we're doing, or to make a more radical shift in our career or life. Knowing, and being ready for, the degree of upheaval is essential, before we launch into the changes ahead. We need to be sure that we'll have the resilience to go the full distance and make a safe landing.

Many of us will be working for large companies, and there might be scope to make our change internally, or else move to another firm. Most careers will be a blend of internal job changes (within an existing employer) and external (to a different organisation).

Promotions, restructuring and career opportunities will present themselves throughout our tenure in any given job. Whether or not they mean a change in job title or remuneration, change is still change. Indeed, many of us decide that it's time to go, exactly because those internal changes have slowed down, or dried up altogether.

"If you want small changes in your life, work on your attitude. But if you want big and primary changes, work on your paradigm."

Stephen Covey
Educator, author, businessman

Job change is how our careers develop and advance. Statistics on internal change are very poorly documented, and riddled with definitional problems, so let's just assume that we'll experience some of these in our careers, and deal with them as they occur. External change is more visible, and reflects the statistics shown above. So the question is, in part: 'Is it time for a local change or time to go?'

More detailed focus on the available information shows that baby boomers (those born between 1946 and 1964) changed jobs as many as 10 times, when they were between eighteen and forty years old, and that the changes accelerated after that age. But within that, 2006 data suggests that they 'enjoyed' at least three different whole careers during their working lives (New York University's School of Continuing and Professional Studies, 2006).

So, increasingly, 'time to go' actually means 'time for radical change'.

It's an open question whether the so-called Gen-Ys and Millennials even want a career. Of course, they are just beginning their forty-odd years at work, and perhaps notions of stability and longevity haven't cropped up yet. But it's clear that they do have a very different expectation of work.

For these groups, work needs to be centred around them and they appear to be less willing to accept major compromises in their expectations. If things are working well for them, they'll stay. If not, then they'll be off. They appear to be less bound by loyalty, or duty to stay.

And let's be honest, younger people tend to be cheaper to employ and be more enthusiastic if they're engaged in what they're doing. They become very attractive to potential employers.

At present, employers and employees appear to be willing to continue the churn. It remains to be seen if job-hopping will continue, as they get older.

Age also matters with older workers, too.

We've seen discrimination based on race, gender and sexual orientation, throughout our working lives, and action is increasing to combat it. But the new kid on the discrimination block is age.

One survey, of the over-60s segment in America, found that almost eighty per cent reported having experienced ageism. The incidents which they reported included other people making assumptions - like they were physically impaired or suffered memory loss as a result of their age.

Perhaps more alarmingly, there is the 'double whammy' of older workers having to work longer before retirement, yet not receiving any investment in training or development. This is usually because employers believe that older workers will be retiring before they see the return on that investment.

A study, by Duke University in the United States, revealed that the most common type of ageism (reported by 31 per cent of respondents) was being entirely ignored, or not being taken seriously, as a result of their age. Their views were deemed out of date, or the person was no longer considered sufficiently creative, or dynamic. In other words, experience is side-lined in favour of exciting new changes with younger employees.

In these environments, life becomes intolerable in the workplace and older workers decide that it's time to go. In their case, it really does feel like quitting, because it's more about 'anywhere but here' instead of 'onwards and upwards'. Even for them, I'd recommend turning the situation to a positive forward outlook, not a negative retrospective one.

If we do decide to go, it's worth looking at who's hiring. We may be in a corporate career today, but that might not continue. As of 2010, the U.S. Small Business Administration reported that small businesses were the largest employers – in fact, nearly 98 per cent of employers were small businesses. Between 2009 and 2011, when the economy took a downturn, small businesses created more than two-thirds of all new jobs.

The emergence of small businesses might seem like the way for more mature job seekers to go. The hunger for talent of the smaller enterprise can offer a good landing place for older workers and their experience. But the higher rate of business failures, at the smaller end of town, can increase the frequency of voluntary and involuntary departures

This also means, of course, an acceleration in the rate at which workers are changing jobs.

"Oh, I'm all about small business. I think what we've learned from big business and big Wall Street is that unchecked greed and the creation of false value gets us all in trouble. If we look at the American economy, who's really creating value? It's the small businesses."

Robert Herjavec
Businessman, investor, author, broadcaster

So, is this the point to consider a downscaling to a smaller employer, or even going it alone in our own small business?

If we go to smaller companies, behaviour is likely to be much more driven by personalities and relationships. The 'softer' skills, and personal interaction, might become more important than ever.

Questions of longevity disappear and being seen to deliver personal value becomes more immediate. Adaptability, flexibility and resilience will be our best allies.

On a personal note, about four years ago I decided that it was 'time to go' from my corporate job and made exactly that change. I founded Epiphanies Life Strategy & Coaching, I became self-employed and I've never been happier.

Working for myself was at the ultimate end of the downsizing spectrum, but it has brought with it huge joys.

Creativity, freedom, self-determination and operational nimbleness were always in my personal make-up, and this gave me the opportunity to exercise them, under my own control. I feel liberated.

However, it also brings enormous risk - business, financial and even reputational risk now confronts me on a daily basis. Every decision is tempered by a balance between my own sense of purpose and basic survival. But that's OK.

Even if it's a knife-edge, at least it's my knife-edge.

Both risk and reward are highly personal and when it goes well there's nothing more liberating. When it's less certain, it can feel excruciating.

"Even if you fall on your face, you're still moving forward."

Victor Kiam,
Entrepreneur, Remington Products (spokesperson)
New England Patriots football team owner

Change also comes into our lives away from work.

Many of us aspire to a happy married life. Those who achieve it will tell us that the keys to success are not only about growing individually, but with each other; facing adversity and setbacks together and being prepared to accept the foibles of the partner with equanimity.

Sadly, the Western world is faced with a divorce rate of around 50 per cent, where couples cite 'irreconcilable differences', personal abuse, infidelity or other external circumstances.

But is it that simple? Can they realistically blame anything, or anyone, other than themselves? I suspect that they came into marriage with unrealistic expectations of how much effort, flexibility and adaptability it would take to make it work. Yes, there's that word resilience again. Not toughness, resilience.

Of course, in an adversarial legal contest, divorcees are rarely encouraged to take the responsibility upon themselves. They may capitulate as the 'guilty' party, but they will hold on to a blaming mindset in many cases.

Then, with the divorce and its external factors out of the way, they step right back into the next marriage. More than 60 per cent of divorcees remarry and again, 50 per cent of those marriages end in divorce. The cycle is destined to occur over and over until each individual is prepared to take responsibility for their own decisions and outlook.

Our bodies are also in a state of constant change that can, in turn, bring big changes in our lives. Statistics around the prevalence of permanent disability vary but the consensus is that about 80 per cent of such disability cases occur after birth. Relatively few disabilities are present at birth. Illness, accidents and infirmity can happen to anyone and, of course, bring about enormous changes in our lives.

And let's not forget about mental illness or infirmity.

It's believed that about 40 per cent of us will suffer a period of mental illness in our lives, ranging from mild to severe. For 25 per cent it will become a chronic or recurring impairment.

During a period of mental or emotional illness, we can endure, or even cause, huge changes in our lives, which can have permanent effects, even after the episode has passed.

It's at those times, of physical or mental injury, that our personal resilience is severely tested. They're also the times when support networks, and willingness to be supported, become essential parts of our lives.

None of us wants to become disabled in any way, but we would do well to guard against it. Physical and mental fitness help us to survive short-term challenges, and a strong fund of resilience will help us to face them with a more positive frame of mind. Also, it might be too late to reach out to others when the crisis occurs. We should be building and maintaining personal support systems throughout our life, well before any big change happens.

"When you have a dream that you can't let go of, trust your instincts and pursue it. But remember, real dreams take work. They take patience, and sometimes they require you to dig down very deep. Be sure you're willing to do that."

Harvey Mackay
Businessman, author, columnist

So let's get into the right mindset about change, and let's do it today.

If everything changes, there's no point in trying to hunker down and hope that it will pass us by – it won't. What's more, life begins at the edge of our comfort zone. So, if we want to live up to our true purpose, we need to be willing to push the boundaries of our comfort zone, and start to live life to the fullest. After all, if change is coming, we might as well make it change for the better; change that suits our own purpose.

What's more, if we're going to drive change, there's no point in changing for more of the same. We all have the potential to be greater than we are today, so we simply can't settle for 'just enough', when that little 'extra' could bring us closer to our purpose.

Our purpose is calling - knowing that we're moving towards it will help to keep us strong, and on track, through the changes to come.

It's our purpose in life that really matters. Sometimes it's hard to know what our true purpose is, but it's really easy to notice when we're not living it!

The things in our life, which we've valued so highly, are really just 'stuff'. Although we get really attached to the material things, they're not what matters most and they do not define us. Purpose, not 'stuff', builds resilience and fulfilment.

"You don't need strength to let go of something. What you really need, is understanding."

Guy Finley
Writer, philosopher, and spiritual teacher

Most of us can make do with much less than we think we need. When it's time to change, it's a good time to leave 'stuff' behind. More importantly, it's time to let go of our attachment to 'stuff' and move closer to our purpose. We were made to do great things, and if we're not achieving them where we are, then it really is time to go.

It's time to decide what our purpose is and move towards it.

In the same way as 'stuff', we accumulate people who are simply not good for us.

We instinctively know them - the negative, back-biting critics. We also know, in our hearts, that their opinion of us is none of our business, it's all about theirs!

There's a cruel expression about 'taking out the trash' when referring to moving things and people out of our lives. It's not that they've become trash, in any absolute sense. Everything and everyone has intrinsic value, which carries on through time. It might simply be that we no longer need their contributions in our lives.

In particular, there's no need to carry them forward, into our new lives, if they will no longer serve us there. Thinking of them as 'trash' is demeaning to them, and draining on us. Merely acknowledge the value that they once held for us, recognise that value has ended and gently let them go.

"We must let go of the life we have planned so as to accept the one that is waiting for us."

Joseph Campbell
Writer and lecturer; comparative mythology and religion

When it's time to go, there will be only a few people we'll really want to keep in our lives, if any. Of course, other people can be a help at times of change, but only if we're sure that they align, and support, our vision of that change. This is one time when we should keep our thoughts to ourselves, until we're sure of the people around us. Our networks will come in handy later, once we've decided whether, where and when to go.

Now is the time to take a moment, and list the few people who really matter to us, the rest can be moved into the 'no longer' pile.

Yes, they'll judge us, whether we stay or go, so we should get ready to shrug off their opinions. Be ready for the judgments, but stick to our instincts, despite their views.

Even close friends and colleagues are likely to chatter about our dissatisfaction or plans, when we're thinking that it's time to go. They probably mean well, but their gossip can be distracting, and even harmful. So let's keep our ideas to ourselves, for now.

When it is time for the big change, everything will already be in flux and life will become even less predictable. This is the time for us to embrace our 'inner gymnast'. We'll need to be flexible in our attitude to nearly everything – job, home, life's contents, status, relocation, finances.

"Every day is a new day, and you'll never be able to find happiness if you don't move on."

Carrie Underwood,
Country music singer, songwriter, actress

It's not other people's job to carry us, or our purpose; it's ours.

We know that the time ahead will be shaky, and even a little fearful. It's our own resolve and resilience that will get us through, when it's time to go.

So, before any big change, we need to take time to truly understand what's driving us towards a new future, rather than away from a troubled present or past.

Consider just how locked in we are to the present. Consider all of our trappings of success and status. Consider the 'must haves', the 'nice to haves' and the 'don't cares'.

The bigger we can make the 'don't care' list, the more degrees of freedom we will allow ourselves in the big change.

Even being clear about the precise time to go will count.

"Yesterday is not ours to recover, but tomorrow is ours to win or lose."

Lyndon B. Johnson
(former) President of United States of America

A vision is a daydream with a shape, a goal is a vision with a deadline and a plan is a goal with some actions and resources.

So when it's time to go, it's time to make a plan.

We can decide what needs to be done and when and how to do those things.

If it's time to go, it's time to get real.

The next chapter will explore some of those practical considerations of the move.

Remember to download your free

Resilience

Workbook

Just follow the link below.

http://mikegordonbooks.com/download-siq-workbook/

You'll need the password that you find, at the end of Chapter 12

CHAPTER 11: MAKE THE MOVE

> "The world is changing very fast. Big will not beat small any more. It will be the fast beating the slow."
>
> **Rupert Murdoch**
> **Media proprietor**

By now we've reached the crunch point and we're all set to make a move.

We've learned all we can here, we've grown as much as we're going to and we've tolerated as much as we're prepared to take.

It might be a big or a small move, but remember, it's never quitting. It's change.

So let's make it a change to a better place; onward and upward.

Actually, we're still not done yet. If we're going to make the move, we need to make it successfully.

There are still a number of considerations to bear in mind, that will help us move carefully and land safely.

This chapter is a checklist of ideas to cover as we do it. Let's go!

Moving for money

Let's say we're changing jobs and we've secured a 10 per cent rise in pay. Could we have negotiated that increase where we are? It's never too late to renegotiate our terms at our current job.

There's nothing like a firm offer from a new employer to make our present boss pay more attention. If money is the sole issue, perhaps they would be willing to match the offer to keep you happy and stay.

It's always worth a try.

"I think a lot of times it's not money that's the primary motivation factor; it's the passion for your job and the professional and personal satisfaction you get out of doing what you do that motivates you."

Martin Yan
Chef and food writer

Not every job change is all about money, but it does help. So, as we make the move, we may want to consider what that '10 percent more' really means.

It's a good idea to compare like for like, when looking at the money. It always pays to do the arithmetic.

A rise in responsibility will often require longer hours. Simply divide the new salary by the new hours that are expected.

I'm often amazed at how quickly an 'increase' can end up being an effective pay cut, when the time dimension is introduced to the equation.

Consider, if we lose out on time-based payments for uncapped hours, 15 per cent extra hours for a 10 per cent salary increase is actually going backwards.

Never be afraid to measure the full benefit or cost, when considering a move.

This includes the possibility of losing out on things like holiday entitlements, seniority levels or stock/share options, as well as just hours expected.

It might be worth 10 per cent in hard cash today, but it will also change our working conditions.

We need to ensure that the new payment fully compensates us for the extra responsibility and effort. Don't just look at the salary being offered, in isolation.

There's usually more to be considered than the simple dollars and cents.

What about the longer term?

We need to be sure that the promotions will keep coming, and that there is still room for growth. Otherwise the 10 per cent soon becomes eroded. Before long, we end up worse off, in real terms.

When considering the financial gain of any move, it's important to look ahead, to the real monetary impact on our lives.

Remember, we're probably working to live, so let's be clear that we're still going to have a life after the move.

Beware of the counter-offensive

It's odd that, when we announce our intention to leave, we suddenly become much more 'valuable' to those around us.

That's when the counter-offers get wheeled out. They might come from our present employers - offering promotions, pay rises, a bigger office, or a smarter car - or maybe our co-workers suddenly turn on the charm offensive. They respond to their own sense of impending loss and try to head it off. Suddenly, we've become indispensable and they can't imagine carrying on without us.

"The whole Obama phenomenon brings up memories from my distant past: the good-looking guy who talks real good, whose line you don't buy immediately but whose charm is so dazzling that he gradually convinces you that this time it will be different."

Marianne Williamson
Spiritual teacher, author and lecturer

If these people really did value us, the pay, the promotions, the benefits and the charm would already be there. If we were already feeling that appreciation, our desire to move probably wouldn't have surfaced, or at least we'd already have factored it in to our decision. It wasn't, so how real is it now?

It's all very interesting but we have already decided to make the move, for our own reasons.

Sudden declarations of commitment are probably too little, too late. Band-Aid offers are usually only skin deep. They might last for a short while but they're rarely a cure for what ails us.

We can review the offers, by all means, but they no longer deserve the 'inside track', in the two-horse race between current and future opportunities.

Thank you doesn't jingle

There are always financial implications when we move. In today's world, there is often a redundancy programme we can hook into. Or we might be entitled to severance pay.

There's no reason to leave for free, if there is some extra cash circulating. Don't forget that there might be unclaimed holiday/long-service pay.

If we're expecting a bonus in the next pay cycle it might be worth our while to stick around to harvest what's owed to us. It's a good idea to time our exit, and make sure that any bonus actually lands, before we go.

Even if it means hanging on a little longer, it could well be worth it to wait until that extra money falls from the tree.

Also, in the long term, there's the question of our retirement fund.

What happens to our pension/superannuation/401(k) entitlements?

If it starts from scratch, there could be a knock-on to its future value by the time we retire. A fragmented fund is often worth less than a single fund and can hurt us in the long term.

"But, at the end of the day, we need to represent the taxpayers who have made enormous sacrifices. Many have lost their jobs. Many of them have seen their companies - they don't have a pension - they have seen their companies cut the match for their 401(k). They have seen their health care benefits be shredded."

John Kasich
US Governor (Ohio) 2010, 2014

Dig out our existing contract and terms, before making any decision, and ensure that we claim everything to which we are entitled.

If it's complicated, speak to a lawyer or financial adviser.

If we're leaving, leave well

We might have been unhappy but it never serves us well to burn bridges. Here are three good reasons to leave a smooth path behind us.

1. Our reputation is our strongest asset

We shouldn't be leaving any reasons for bad-mouthing after the move. In a connected world, our reputation will follow us and can help us into the future. Equally, it could come around to bite us later.

Bad behaviour during any change is likely to be the last thing that people remember and might end up defining their opinion of us for ever.

"It takes many good deeds to build a good reputation, and only one bad one to lose it."

Benjamin Franklin
USA founding father 1706-1790

We should aim to ensure that our immediate, and extended, networks are viewing our move with only positive sentiments, so that they will continue to endorse us ,as we go forward and our new world will be happier to welcome us.

2. Self-respect is critical

After the dust settles, we'll still be us. So far, we've played the game with integrity and honour. Now is not the time to tarnish our own sense of self-respect with some ill-judged remarks to those we're leaving behind.

Make the move with dignity and professionalism.

Our friends and allies will be delighted with our new opportunities and we should embrace their support during the transition. If it helps, we can retain compassion for those we're leaving behind. After all, we're moving on to bigger and better things and they are staying put. Be generous to those we choose to leave and loyal to those we want to hold on to.

Remember back to my own example. I was glad to be leaving. I felt compassion for those remaining in that environment and I had opportunities stretching our ahead of me. In an odd way, I felt like the power was in my hands, even if the other side was playing out their separation 'ritual'.

3. Leave the door open

Just because the situation we're leaving has less value for us now, than it once might have had, doesn't mean that there is no residual value left there at all. We were once successful there and our success will have been noted by a few good people.

As we move forward, there may be moments when that residual value will come in handy once more. In particular, some of the people that we knew might still be helpful to us. It might be no more than the odd phone call or text message, or a chat over a coffee, but they still have the potential to share value with us. Perhaps it's something they knew how to do, that we can still learn from, or an interesting perspective that can make us see things differently. Maybe we even want to entice them to join us in our new lives.

As we move forward, into uncertainty, it can be reassuring that we have a few people from our past who still have our back. Maintaining the link with them is good for our morale, our ongoing value and, of course, our resilience.

So let's not be slamming the door behind us. Let's not burn all the bridges back to earlier value, regardless of how tempting it is in the excitement or heat of a change. Maintaining the link always has the potential to bring us continuing value, even if we can't see it right now.

Make the transition as smooth as possible

Why make life tough? As soon as we say we're moving, our so-called 'best' friends can quickly turn to enemies. Jealousy, resentment, or a sense of rejection, can quickly surface, as soon as we indicate our intentions.

We should be aiming to leave a well-ordered environment and that will probably require co-operation from those around us. We'll need their support, so we shouldn't alienate them during the final days. Don't give them any reason to sabotage us, as we make the move.

Have a script

Lots of people around us; in our old firm, social friends, family, and even new co-workers, will want to know the gossip, the 'inside' story.

The world has become accustomed to soap operas, but our own lives don't need to be one for other people.

It's a good idea to have the script ready for these occasions. There are some trusty old phrases to consider here: new opportunities; more challenges; more time with the kids; an easier commute; and many others.

Be sure that they have a strong element of truth, because insincerity is easy to spot and can jeopardise goodwill in an instant.

As a starting point, we can build a script around 'why, what and how' we're making the change.

These three positive elements will make an interesting and compelling story about the move.

"The stumbling steps to becoming real, is the only script that's really worth following in this world or the one that's coming."

Brennan Manning
Author, priest, and public speaker

Writing them down will help to shape it and will also help you to remember the responses. Even practise saying them out loud so that they become natural.

Staying positive will enhance our own sense of wellbeing and leave a better reputation with others. In short, keep it clear, positive and compelling. Let's write the script.

Not going the extra mile

The only extra mile we should be going is the one out, up and away. Our whole focus should be on closing things, not opening them or fixing long-term systemic inadequacies. That's probably why we've decided to leave in the first place.

Yes, we should be ensuring a smooth handover, to whoever is taking on our case load. That's an honourable and professional practice.

But now is not the time to reclassify the company filing system or rewrite the procedures manual. And it's certainly not the time to be starting any new long-term projects or campaigns.

> *"I don't like paying too much for anything or wasting it. I think that I'm more of a balanced individual."*

John Caudwell
Founder, UK Phones 4u, philanthropist

A common demand, from bosses who are losing us, runs something like *'I can't release you until...'* We can all fill in the blanks, but typically it will include the complete backlog of unfinished work, plus a number of the things that nobody has paid attention to for years.

No, they are no longer our responsibility.

We should be doing all that we reasonably can, so that our departure creates no extra collateral damage, but, after all, we're about to leave all of the chaos and progress to a new set of challenges.

Exit politely

Employers, or those we're leaving, often expect an exit interview - and that can be full of traps. It's reasonable for them to want to know why we're going and that we've left everything in good order. But that's it!

This is not the time to vent pent-up emotions, nor leak competitive information about our new position.

We should make the move for good reasons and that's all we need to share. It's great if we're able to give constructive feedback about our time with them.

Even showing gratitude for the time and opportunities that we've had will help smooth our exit.

The time for deep and searching discussion has passed. There was once an opportunity for engagement, but that has gone. The break should be clean and with minimal explanation, justification or acrimony.

Clear the decks

Now is a good time to go through our systems and remove all our personal stuff. Delete personal emails, calendar appointments, notes, documents, files and folders.

Chances are, our current employer will simply wipe our systems behind us, but they might not. We don't really want diary entries, secret assignations, love notes, or draft resumes lying around for others to find, copy, or even share around.

So when it's time to go, it's wise to clean up behind ourselves.

Take our stuff with us

How many times have we seen people do the 'walk of shame' with their sad little box of personal possessions? Frankly, our time at the old place has been more than a pot plant, a stapler and a photo of the kids. Our worth is measured in the things we did, the things we created and the value we generated.

I'm certainly not advocating that we steal company secrets or intellectual property; far from it... don't do that!

But it is perfectly acceptable to harvest our experience and learning from the job when we leave.

There's no law against capturing the memories of what we've done and what we learned. Our experience is what we're being hired for now, and in the future, and it forms part of our personal heritage.

"Stealing is stealing. I don't care if it's on the Internet, or you're breaking into a warehouse somewhere - it's theft."

Patrick Leahy
US senator (Vermont)

Most places have a sense of ownership, and even copyright, to the work we did with them.

Taking the details of those items could even be a criminal offence.

Nevertheless, how we worked, our approach, and our creativity, is ours. We can't take customer files with us, but, if we had personal relationships, they can endure after the move.

Be careful about non-compete clauses, but there is no such thing as non-relate conditions.

People work with people, and that prevails over time, regardless of where and how we worked together.

Sweet talk or commitments

In a buoyant market, prospective employers will make all sorts of promises, to land the right candidate.

When making the move, it's in our best interests to make sure that those promises are written down. So check the contract, terms and conditions, and job description, to make sure that all of the promises are included.

That way, a new employer can be held accountable for what was verbally pledged. It's too late to renegotiate, once we've signed on the dotted line - simply don't do so, until everything agreed is locked down.

Take professional advice if it gets complicated, but do check the fine print. This is real life, not Google or Facebook terms, to be overlooked or put in the 'too hard' basket.

Read the signs

Not everything can be written into a contract, but the news about our new situation is already out there.

LinkedIn, Google and the 'blogosphere' are good sources of advance information when considering a move.

Check out the 'word on the street' about the new company, the job and even our new bosses. Read what the industry is talking about and any general feedback from the current employees.

If there's a sudden explosion of lay-offs, or disgruntled ex-employees, then the internal picture might not be as rosy as it's being presented.

Forewarned is forearmed. Even if there is some uncomfortable news out there, it always helps to move forward with our eyes wide open.

Land gently

In coming to rest in our new place, let's land with care. Let's remember, our new employers have hired us because they think we're a good deal; the best of the bunch.

So there's no immediate need to over perform from day one.

Our move was always intended to be purposeful and we should make sure all of those promises really have turned into commitments. We can check that the reality matches up to the undertakings. Of course, it won't be exactly like we imagined, but it needs to be close enough.

If it's not, now is the time to call it out. If we let it slide, the window for discussion could close very quickly.

There are new procedures, people and politics in the new place. Learning to navigate them is part of our own settling-in responsibilities, no one else's.

Remember, we will have a honeymoon period for the 'new kid' to adjust to 'how things are done around here'. So let's use it!

Our arrival is when expectations of immediate performance are at the lowest they'll ever be.

It's easier to impress at that point, than at any time later, once expectations have mounted. It's an opportunity to use this slack to watch and learn.

It's good to get a few early 'wins' chalked up, and to build confidence within the new community. As much as possible, these should be relatively short-term, straight-forward achievements and be fairly visible to the new employers and bosses. Having people see our worth early will pay dividends in the longer term.

It's OK for the newbie to ask questions... even 'dumb' ones. It's a golden opportunity to gather evidence and to learn the real layout of the new place.

It's not just about the photocopier, the coffee machine or washrooms. It's more than the operational processes. It should be mostly about the people, and how they operate together. We've been given the opportunity to step back, observe, ask questions and draw some conclusions. Let's do just that.

"Upon arriving, meeting their teachers and signing up for classes, these students began to realise that their attendance at Delaware State University was not a goal achieved, but rather a dream being sown - a first step, if you will."

Michael N Castle
US Governor (Delaware)

Take the time to observe, process what we see, learn how the new place works and choose how we want to engage with it. In particular, this is a great time to do some people watching.

As a relative outsider, it's easier to see how people relate to their work, to each other, and to us, before we become embedded in the environment. Getting to know the people and learning what makes them tick will pay dividends in the long term.

This is a good place to remember about our left, right and centre minds.

People make the world go round and we're encountering a whole new set of people. And that's complicated.

So let's not overthink it too soon. Look for signs of behaviour to feed our left mind.

Watch how relationships work among others and towards us.

Use our right mind to spot the fertile ground and the potential traps.

Most importantly, we need to trust the centre mind; our 'gut' feeling. Our instincts are highly tuned during change, and this is no time to ignore them.

If something doesn't feel right, it probably isn't. If we get that uneasy caution, no matter how unspecific it might be, we should be paying attention.

We can be guided by our centre mind to seek out more tangible evidence, to help our left and right minds draw some conclusions.

After all, it's not called a honeymoon period for nothing.

The settling-in period is all about becoming comfortable... with each other.

Change isn't about the good and bad things that happen to us. It's about how we behave in these situations. It's about what we do next that really shows our resilience.

When we choose to leave, we're actually choosing to arrive at a new place.

The landing is ours to make safe and easy, or difficult. Either way, it's our choice.

This chapter has looked at ways to make the transition and landing easier. I also hope that it's demonstrated that it never needs to be about quitting.

It's all about change and placing change under our own control.

It's our own life and we have the right to make decisions and act in our own best interests. Of course, we're not islands and everything we do will have an impact on those around us.

So, let's change.

Let's move on.

But let's do it carefully and considerately.

Remember to download your free

Resilience
Workbook

Just follow the link below.

http://mikegordonbooks.com/download-siq-workbook/

You'll need the password that you find, at the end of Chapter 12

CHAPTER 12: MAKE SENSE OF IT ALL

"If you live long enough, you'll make mistakes. But if you learn from them, you'll be a better person. It's how you handle adversity, not how it affects you. The main thing is never quit, never quit, never quit."

William J. (Bill) Clinton
(Former) President, United States of America

We've covered a lot of ground, and met a wealth of ideas, on the whole subject of quitting or changing things in life.

I'm guessing it's been a lot to digest and maybe we haven't absorbed it all.

That's OK. Take time, go back and review the important bits and consider how it impacts on our lives individually.

Big changes are never easy and they shouldn't be undertaken lightly.

So it's worth taking the time to pick out the pieces that make most sense to each of us, as they relate to our own situations, and our own lives.

Once we've mastered the immediate priorities, we can always go back and pick up the next set of actions. Rome wasn't built in a day, and neither will we be.

There have been a number of recurring themes, which pop up through the book, and it's good to pull these out and summarise them for easier consideration. To help identify the big lessons, this chapter will draw out the high-level themes, and lay them out in a logical and easy-to-follow structure.

I've grouped them into three main sections that should help you to consider each in its context.

- Quitting is never really quitting

- Follow the value

- Take action and change successfully

Quitting is never really quitting

When things pile up, we often think about quitting, but is that the best option? In fact, is it ever really an option at all?

1. Change, not quitting

Life goes on, even if our situations change. As soon as we step out of one space, we step straight into another.

Life has no pauses, no do-overs and there's no waiting room in which to hang out while life changes for us.

So recognise that leaving one place is actually moving forward to another.

We might as well choose where we're moving to, instead of simply running away from where we are.

2. Take a breath

No matter how pressured we feel, there's always time to step back and take control of our reactions.

Acting in haste is usually a ticket to disappointment, so we're better off taking a moment to cool down and collect ourselves. We make better decisions when we're cool, calm and collected and we let the surge of adrenaline pass.

So take a breath. In fact, take several long, deep breaths. Count to ten slowly, if that helps.

3. Review the situation

The advantage of stepping back is that it gives us the perspective of the bigger picture.

The noise and chaos of detail can be our worst enemy in times of stress. It drives us into knee-jerk reactions and we often live to regret the things that we do, or say, in the heat of the moment.

Instead, that's the time to remember the full context. Consider why we are in the situation in the first place. Bring to mind the excitement of when we first began and check if it's still there. If small things are getting in the way, we can judge if they are really intolerable, or if we can adjust them a little to let the joy shine through again.

If big things have changed, is it all bad? Maybe the changes are actually better, but we've become too attached to our expectations to see it.

So go back to first principles, of why we're doing what we're doing, and regain a sense of proportion.

4. There are always options

The future holds infinite possibilities and our destinies lie in our own hands.

We can choose to make the best future for ourselves, simply by deciding what that future should be, and taking steps to make it happen.

They might be big steps or small, but they should be purposeful.

So look at all the options, even the impossible ones.

The stronger the desire to quit, the wider our options can be.

After all, if we're in an 'all or nothing' moment, where everything is at stake, the rewards will have to be big enough to merit the risks.

Small gripes probably just need some fine tuning, rather than jumping ship altogether.

5. Make a decision

Simply throwing up all the cards (which is exactly what quitting is) is actually deciding not to make a decision.

It's letting the universe, or dumb luck, make the decision for us. In a world of infinite possibilities, there's very little chance that the best option will be the one to land at random.

We've stepped back, we've reviewed our options. Now is the time to decide which option we'll choose.

Once we've chosen the best option for us, we can then put the wheels in motion to get us there.

Follow the value

Everything we do has some sense of value attached to it. We put in some effort, and we expect some kind of reward for it. It's a simple principle, but we so often forget about it in the hurly-burly of day-to-day life.

So let's look at the value of what we're doing in our lives.

1. Personal values

These are the opposite of received value.

They are the deep-seated drivers, which lie within us and define who we are. They can include the higher feelings of honesty, justice, loyalty, love or fun. They also include the practical aspects like rigour, dependability, learning, quality or wealth.

They vary for each of us, and they might even change over time, as we mature.

Nevertheless, they are deeply ingrained and act as our measuring stick for everything that we do, and everything that goes on around us. Very often we're not even aware of our values, until they are violated. Something happens and we feel it's just not right. We get an uneasy feeling that often gives us those thoughts of quitting.

By understanding our values clearly and explicitly, we have a better chance of moving toward what is good for us and away from what isn't. Certainly, if we know what our values are, we can tell which ones might be being violated, and that will point us in the direction of a solution. So, values are our internal (inside-out) compass, while received value comes from outside, in return for our effort.

2. Balance the value

Everything we do is an exchange of value: value in for value out.

So, as with any exchange, it's useful to check the balance sheet. The rewards that we get, as received value, should balance equally with the effort that we're putting in, as our delivered value.

If we're not receiving enough payback, it's easy to feel cheated and that drives us towards quitting. If we're receiving too much, we're probably depriving someone else, and they'll think about quitting. So resilience and sustainability is all about balance; input for output.

3. Show me the money

The traditional exchange, in the workplace, has been effort for money.

This was typified by an hourly rate, or a piece rate, for the effort being given. Then ideas like overtime, night rates and unsocial hours (so-called penalty rates, in Australia), were introduced, to recognise that not all hours were equal.

We give up our time and effort to get money in exchange, and those hours are carved out from the rest of our lives. Modern workplaces have become more complex and demanding, and it's too easy to let the balance shift. Salaried staff no longer get hourly rates, and are expected to work to a flexible demand. Rush jobs make unusual demands on our free time, and can double our workload, without commensurate pay increases. What might once have been a fair deal, can easily slip into exploitation, and the value is eroded.

So do the maths, and decide if our rewards still match the effort.

4. Money's not everything

Of course, not all rewards have a direct cash value.

We get value simply by being good at the things we're doing. It can be an avenue for our creativity, or our sense of service. Socialising with those around us also brings its own rewards.

So let's not forget to add in the non-financial rewards of whatever we're doing. They're part of the balance and can often be more rewarding than simple cash. But let's not get carried away. Social, emotional or spiritual rewards can also lead us to over-paying, in time and effort.

A sense of duty, responsibility, or indispensability can lead us to giving too much, even for those delightful rewards. It's always all about balance. So never forget to check out the cost, in wear and tear, for what 'soft' rewards we're receiving.

Take action and change successfully

Left, right and centre.

We take action based on our decisions about what's best for us. And we know by now that our best decisions are made when we bring our whole self into the mix.

It'll be important to make our best decisions, about any changes in our lives, and the bigger the change, the more of us we need to bring to it.

We might compare our head, heart and soul to our left, right and centre minds and use all of our resources to make the best decisions.

Separately, they look at the how, what and why of the issue.

1. Deeply centred

Our unconscious minds hold the secrets of who we truly are and what is most fundamental to us.

We might think of this as the soul, or the 'why', of the situation. It starts with our personal values and they quickly drive our passion and our sense of life's purpose.

Living our values, passion and purpose are what will make us truly happy. When we move away from them, we end up disillusioned, despondent and begin thinking of quitting. Unfortunately, those feelings tend to be very unspecific and troubling, often without any tangible or conscious shape to them. Stress, anxiety and frustration are most often the signs that we're off purpose, or violating our values.

Our best guide to understanding ourselves is our intuition, often called our 'gut feeling'. So let's learn to listen to, and trust, our intuition. If things feel right, they probably are; if they don't, then they're probably bad for us. Tuning into our intuition can be difficult in a turbulent world, because of all of the noise and activity that is going on around us. That's why stepping back is so important. I'm a great believer in meditation and mindfulness, as techniques for clearing our minds and letting our intuition emerge.

The old expression of 'sleep on it' is a great way to let our unconscious mind do the work. How often do we wake, to find that last night's problem has fallen back into perspective? My early morning shower is the time when I have my best epiphanies. That's because my unconscious mind has already solved the issues and my conscious mind catches up, when it's fresh and clear. So sit quietly with the big issues and let the truth emerge.

There's no sledgehammer in our unconscious minds.

2. Get the facts

Our left minds love data and love to analyse things.

If we let our mind run away, we end up worrying about things, and tying ourselves in knots. Our centre, unconscious, mind might be giving us one of those uneasy feelings, and the best way of settling ourselves is to bring in our left minds to analyse the situation. So let's feed our left minds with some facts... real facts.

Now is the time to look for tangible evidence of what's actually going on: how many hours, what money is moving in or out, how tired or energised we are, how smoothly the process is operating. All of these are tangible, and measurable, and will give our left minds something to chew on. They are the kind of things we can put into our mental spreadsheets, flow charts or balance sheets. In my consulting days, I used to talk about 'informed' decisions, and they were all about being based on information that was evident and supportable.

Left-minded thinking is based on evidence.

3. Heart of the matter

Our right minds are all about our physical senses, our emotions and our relationships.

Ultimately all decisions have a large emotional component, whether we recognise it or not. It's the 'what' part of the equation, and is where the heart of the matter lies. So let's not be squeamish about involving our emotions and relationships in our biggest decisions.

Our behaviour will soon tell us what our moods are: high-fiving our colleagues, having those air-punching moments of success, walking about whistling or with smiles on our faces.

Or perhaps we're grumpy, irritable or withdrawn.

Which do we prefer?

If a situation is making us unhappy, or placing strain on our relationships, it's time for some changes; changes made where we are, or a larger change, to somewhere new.

But let's be clear, we're talking about longer-term emotional states, what makes us happy or sad overall, rather than those instantaneous moments of exhilaration or anger.

Steady, ongoing, happiness is sustainable and anything less will be a recipe for disaster in the long term.

If we re deciding to change, let's decide on happiness and fulfilment.

4. Make a decision

All the evidence in the world might be interesting but it only becomes important when we use it to make decisions.

We've felt the uneasiness from our unconscious self, and we've refined it, with analysis and understanding from our left and right mind. We've reviewed options and weighed them against each other.

Now, which one is best for us? Stay and adapt our current situation, or move onward and upward to a new environment? Either way, we need to make that choice and create a new conviction of what we're going to do.

Otherwise we stagnate, irritation builds and, eventually, we end up simply wanting to run away from it all.

So let's make some decisions.

5. Take action

Now, finally, it's time to act.

Notice that I'm not saying 'quit'.

Clear, decisive action is nothing like quitting. In fact, it's the exact opposite. By acting decisively on considered options, we are taking command of our situation and our lives.

After all, it's our life and nobody else can live it for us. Equally, nobody else can make it happen for us.

Make a plan of action, and then undertake the actions to fulfil the plan, and reach the goals.

I love the project manager's mantra of

Plan the work: work the plan.

We all get to those points, where enough is enough, and it's simply not working for us. What we do next, in the light of those feelings, is what marks us out as winners and achievers.

So here we are at the conclusion.

We started with that deafening demand to get out of here and the aching question of *'Should I Quit?'*. And now we have a well-considered plan of what we're going to do about our situation - of changing things right here or moving to a better place.

Notice, too, that our moods have shifted. We're no longer tied up with frustration, anger or hopelessness. Instead, we are charged with certainty, assurance and determination.

How great does that feel?

We have laid out many strategies for reviewing our circumstances, and gaining clarity and confidence in how we should tackle a bad position. It's been about taking command of the situation and making it work best for us.

Whether we stay where we are, or move to somewhere new, it's all about change... controlled change, change that we define and implement, to make our situation better... for us.

That conviction to change will draw heavily upon our resilience.

This book has pointed to many ways that we can build our resilience, to handle a turbulent world, and to continue to thrive. In fact, reviewing situations and options, and making informed decisions, are great ways to recharge our resilience. By now, we not only have a clear sense of where we're going, but we also have the determination and agility to make it happen.

Yet merely reading this book is not enough.

This guidance has been positioned fairly generically so that it can apply to any circumstance. Now is the time to get specific, and to channel what we've learned, directly into our own unique challenges.

That's why I've created the Resilience Workbook. It's a free resource, for you to use, to develop specific insights for you.

Follow the link at the end of any chapter, and download your own free copy. You'll find individual worksheets, related to each chapter's lessons, so that you can work methodically, to harvest the learning from every one, specifically for yourself.

Choose the chapters and worksheets that resonate most with you and work through them. Start with the obvious ones, and gradually work forward or backwards to complete the full set.

By the time you've completed the full workbook, you'll be in no doubt about what's going on, what needs to change and how you're going to make those changes. Clarity, conviction and a plan are waiting for you at the completion of your own personal workbook.

It's been a huge pleasure for me to share some of my insights, and to guide you on this journey of discovery. As a professional mentor and coach, my personal mission is to help people switch on their own light bulbs; to bring clarity, and to encourage meaningful change.

But none of that is worth anything without real action.

So take action.

Go on.

Be decisive and invest some time and energy into developing your own life and getting the life that you want.

Take command of your own life... and never, ever, quit.

Remember to download your free

Resilience

Workbook

Just follow the link below.

http://mikegordonbooks.com/download-siq-workbook/

You'll need the password that you find, at the end of Chapter 12

The password that you need, to unlock your workbook is

SIQ12

ABOUT THE AUTHOR

Mike Gordon is a highly experienced mentor and life coach, for individuals and businesses. He is the Founder of Epiphanies Life Strategy & Coaching (http://www.epiphanies.com.au/) and the author of the Life Epiphanies Series.

Born and raised in Scotland, Mike Gordon moved to Sydney, Australia, in 2006, after 35 years in the corporate world, as a Strategic Business Consultant, Global Marketing Director and Executive Coach, that took him all over the world (UK, Europe, USA and Asia).

Over the years, Mike has learned what it takes for us to get the life we want. Mike's own journey to wellbeing, and staying true to his authentic self, has been a progression of one epiphany after another.

Everyone has epiphanies that are based on their own experience. Learning to act upon them is the secret of success.

Mike's had his own tough times, but has found ways to reset the dials and find a better path. He has learned how to assess, design, rebuild and run a fulfilling life. With research, study, professional help and self-practice, Mike has emerged as the whole, balanced person he is now.

The happiest he's ever been.

In 2012, Mike Gordon established Epiphanies Life Strategy & Coaching, a small business delivering coaching and mentoring for people who have reached a turning point in their lives.

It focuses on taking personal responsibility for one's own fulfilment and breakthrough moments - learning to walk the talk authentically.

For Mike, writing the 'Life Epiphanies Series' is a way to bring his personal and professional insights to a wider audience. It's intended to share practical guidance on to how to repair and rebalance our lives and wellbeing.

'Should I Quit?' is the first book in the series and helps readers to find, and stay true to, themselves in turbulent times. It's all about handling change and coming out the other side happier, healthier and wiser. It's about being resilient and never, ever, quitting.

Mike is a fundamentally strategic thinker, with a strong intuitive spirit. He works with clients in a structured manner, with a blend of compassion and care.

He has always believed "If you don't know what's broken, you don't know what to fix."

Mike is continuing this journey in life to help others find their true purpose and to take action and control of their lives.

Connect with Mike

For more information connect with Mike through one of the channels listed below

🌐	www.epiphanies.com.au www.mikegordonbooks.com
f	https://www.facebook.com/mikegordonbooks/ www.facebook.com/epiphanies.au/
🐦	https://twitter.com/epimigo
in	https://www.linkedin.com/in/mike-gordon-83530b10
@	epimigo@gmail.com

Epiphanies Life Strategy & Coaching

"Bringing clarity of vision, and a fresh way of seeing the past and present, as inspiration for the future - then making change happen."

Personalised and uniquely tuned support for:

- Personal or Business Mentoring
- Life Direction and Strategy
- Business Direction and Strategy
- Jump start programmes to initiate change
- Builder programmes to keep change on track
- Short-term or ongoing programmes

I'm fundamentally a strategic thinker with a strongly intuitive spirit. I work with clients in a structured and orderly manner but blend this with a deep sense of compassion, care and intuition. Peoples' problems and challenges are never quite what they seem on the surface and I care enough to get to the truth of the situation.

Mike Gordon, **Founder and Director of Coaching**

YOUR PREVIEW OF MIKE'S NEXT BOOK

The next book in the Life Epiphanies Series from Mike Gordon is:-

GET HAPPINESS:

What happy people do!

Mike says,

"I'm the happiest I've ever been and wondered why.

So I've explored the research, looked at my own behaviour, and that of other happy people.

I know it works, and I've written it down for us all to get our own happiness"

> "We're all exactly as happy as we choose to be. Or we can be."
>
> **Mike Gordon**

Happiness is a learned behaviour and we can all learn to switch it on, at any time we choose. We simply need to learn how to do it.

That's where **"Get Happiness: What happy people do"** comes in.

Mike introduces us to the Three S's - the three types of Happiness:-

- Sensory,
- Social and
- Self-based

and describes how each works.

He offers us a step-by-step guide, to develop and maintain our own happiness - practical, scientifically supported and borne out in the day-to-day behaviour of happy people.

This book is your guide to how to be happy. Right here, right now. In fact, even by picking up this book, you'll probably start feeling happier than you were before. That's because you've decided to invest in your own happiness and are doing something about it.

To be the first to know when

"GET HAPPINESS: -What happy people do"

is available, sign up for Mike's newsletter at

www.mikegordonbooks.com

OTHER BOOKS FROM
DREAMSTONE PUBLISHING

Dreamstone publishes books in a wide variety of categories – here are some of our other bestselling books:-

Get Ranked
The Art of Search Engine Optimisation and
Getting Indexed Fast
(The Website Success Accelerator Teaches...)

By Charly Leetham

The Hero Within
Reinvent Your Life, One New Chapter at a
Time

By Serena Low

"Icebreakers : How to Empower, Motivate and
Inspire Your Team, Through Step-by-Step
Activities That Boost Confidence, Resilience
and Create Happier Individuals"

By Di McMath

All Books available from all Amazon sites and other book stores, and available for Kindle too!

The Father Balance
How YOU, as a Father, can successfully build a career and, at the same time, still keep your marriage and family together !

By Leith Adams

Business Strategy :
12 Steps to Business Sanity
How to Optimize Your Profits and Your Time, Grow Your Business and Get Your Life Back Too!

By Kim Lambert

From The Inside Out:
Breakthrough Strategies for Mastering Your Finances:
What YOU Need to Know NOW to Change Your Relationship with Money and Achieve Financial Freedom

By Linda Binns

Be first to know when our next books
are coming out – sign up for our
newsletter at

http://www.dreamstonepublishing.com